THE IC 814 CAPTAIN'S STORY

Captain Devi Sharan was born in 1962 in Sawant, near Karnal in Haryana. He graduated from Dyal Singh College, Karnal and joined Indian Airlines in 1986. He began flying Airbuses from the late nineties. He was awarded the Conway Safe Skies Award 1999 in Atlanta for his role in resolving the IC 814 hijacking.

He lives in New Delhi with his wife.

Srinjoy Chowdhury is National Affairs Editor with Times Now, one of India's leading television news channels. He grew up in Kolkata, where he studied at La Martinière and Presidency College. He joined *Sunday* magazine in 1984 and then, worked for *The Telegraph* and *The Statesman*. After his first book, *Despatches from Kargil* (Penguin, 1999), he wrote *Flight into Fear* (2000) on the hijacking of IC 814 with Devi Sharan, the plane's captain, and three quiz books for Puffin. 'Tahrir,' about his experiences in Cairo during the Arab Spring, was part of *The Dilemma of Popular Sovereignty in the Middle East* (2013), a collection of essays. His report, 'The View from an Indian Television Newsroom: What Makes Us Different,' was included in *Media at Work in China and India* (2015), by Sage.

He lives in New Delhi.

THE IC 814 CAPTAIN'S STORY

FLIGHT INTO FEAR

Captain Devi Sharan
and Srinjoy Chowdhury

hachette
INDIA

First published in 2000 by Penguin India
This edition published in 2024 by Hachette India
(Registered name: Hachette Book Publishing India Pvt. Ltd)
An Hachette UK Company
www.hachetteindia.com

1

ISBN (Paperback) 978-93-5731-475-6

Hachette Book Publishing India Pvt. Ltd
4th/5th Floors, Corporate Centre,
Plot No. 94, Sector 44, Gurugram 122003, India

Typeset in MrsEavesSmartLigRoman
by Mukul

Printed and bound in India by
Manipal Technologies Limited

MIX
Paper | Supporting responsible forestry
FSC™ C043100
FSC www.fsc.org

For all those who prayed for the safe return of the passengers and crew of IC 814. For my passengers and crew, the families of the hostages, my wife Navneet, a pillar of strength during the crisis, and my children. And the people of India.

— Captain Devi Sharan

For Kaushiki Chowdhury

— Srinjoy Chowdhury

Contents

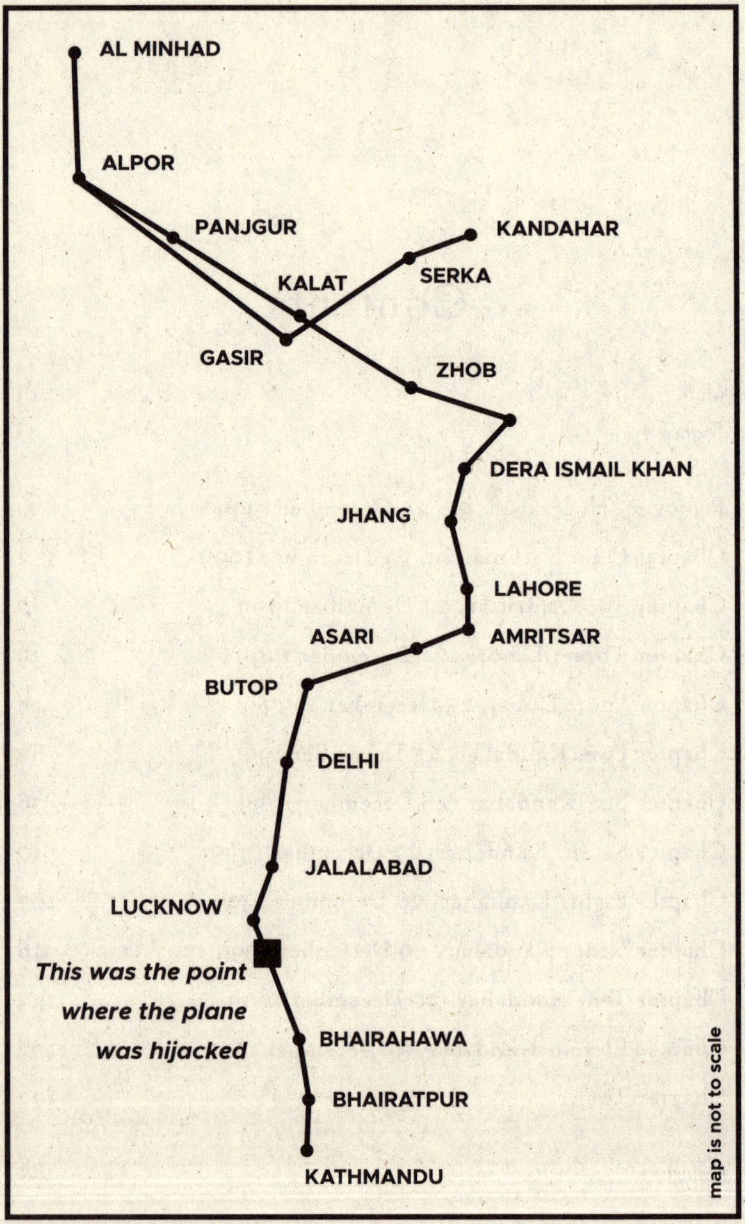

Flight path of IC 814.

Preface

How did all this begin? Well, with a telephone call, some days after the nightmare at Kandahar ended. The phones were ringing all day then. Relieved family and friends called; happy I had returned. One call was by Mr M.K. Bahl. I didn't know him then. 'Why don't you write a book?' he asked.

I would, I decided. I would tell the real story of the hijacking of IC 814. It isn't my story. It is 'our' story, a week in the life of the passengers, the crew and the men responsible for our plight – the hijackers. I would tell the story as I saw it, of what I did, heard and felt. It is a tale of raw fear and acute discomfort, of grief and courage, of hope, and finally, the glory of freedom. There were many moments when I thought I would die.

I spent the early part of those nightmarish hours in the cockpit, on the wrong side of a pistol, flying a plane, knowing that the lives of 188 people depended on my instincts and training. Kandahar was about survival techniques and diplomacy. And about keeping calm and waiting. And waiting. How else can you live with the enemy?

There were other actors in the drama, people I didn't know much about: the Indian government and security agencies, the Taliban, the Pakistan government, the families of the passengers and the crew.

This book is an attempt to tell the whole story as I saw it. I must thank my wife Navneet for dredging up my memories, and my co-author Srinjoy Chowdhury for putting it all together. I also want to thank the passenger on the plane from whose video some of the photographs are taken. There will always be terrorists, and a plane full of innocent people will always be a target. But there is always room for hope and courage, and that is why I want to tell people how we survived. Maybe there is a lesson for us all somewhere.

New Delhi *Captain Devi Sharan, July 2000*

Prologue

Hyderabad

23–24 December 1999

The day before a hijacker burst into the cockpit of the A300 I was flying and waved his pistol at me, I was in Hyderabad, buying pearls for my wife.

'Navneet,' I said to my wife as we entered the gilt-and-glass emporium where the showcases twinkled with precious stones. 'Buy whatever you want. I have a lot of money on me.' The Hyderabad morning glowed with dreamy promise. We were visiting friends in Hyderabad. I would buy my wife pearls. I would take my daughters Aashna, aged eight, and Deeksha, aged eleven, swimming. And we were looking forward to a desert Christmas—cottonwool snow and mistletoe in exciting Sharjah.

This is the best of times and I have earned it, I thought. 'I want the finest pearls for my wife,' I told the girl behind the mirrored counter. I liked a chunky six-string pearl necklace, but Navneet wanted something simpler, a single string of white pearls. I noticed a luminous double string, with a hint of pastel pink and shiny-perfect in the neon glow of the store.

'It won't go with everything. It's not necessary,' Navneet said, alarmed by the extravagance.

'No, it's wonderful. It will suit you,' I overruled her. 'If there's anything else you want, tell me now.'

We bought two sets—the necklace of pink pearls with a matching bracelet and earrings, and a similar set in lustrous white. As our daughters looked at the pearls in the blue velvet cases, they became a little restive.

'Papa, you're buying everything for Mama, nothing for us,' Aashna said. I promised to make amends: a swim in the hotel pool in the afternoon, and ice cream at dinner. In the chill of Kandahar, the brown barren peaks all around, I would remember the expansive warmth of the evening, the rich flavor of the Hyderabadi biryani and the gentle laughter of my children.

When I woke up on Christmas Eve, I had no premonition that my life was going to change forever. I checked out in the grey half-light of dawn, after saying goodbye to my wife. The children were still asleep. I ordered breakfast for them before I checked out. I was going to see them later that evening in Hyderabad. I was flying to New Delhi and then on to Kathmandu and back. I wasn't supposed to be flying the A300 to Kathmandu that day; but we were short of pilots. The pilot on duty cried off for some reason and I was called on 22 December, late in the evening, and told I had to go. Such a change in the duty roster isn't abnormal at all; it happens all the time.

Even after many years of flying, I still get excited about it and don't mind the sacrifices it entails. I love flying, though I never wanted to be an airline pilot. I wanted to join the Indian Air Force (IAF). That had been my dream as a child when I attended the village school in Sawant, Haryana, and later when I was a student in Shahbad. After that, I studied in Dyal Singh College, Haryana. I also joined the National Cadet Corps (NCC) in 1982 and after passing the Pilot Aptitude Battery Test (PABT), got myself sixty hours of flying lessons. So, my life during the college years was physics and chemistry in the morning and flying or farming in the afternoon.

My family thought I was mad—studying science and learning how to fly. No one in our family had done anything like this before. I am the youngest in my family—I have three brothers and two sisters. People in my village pointed at me and said, '*Yeh science padega*? (He'll study science?)' The flying bit had them even more surprised. They said, '*Hamara baccha pagal ho gaya.* (Our kid is mad.)' It was not easy combining so many activities. Karnal, where the flying school was located, was a thirty-kilometre Haryana Roadways bus-ride away. But I was determined to achieve my dreams and to show them I could do it.

I still remember my first solo flight. I had trained for sixteen hours on a Pushpak and now, I would be on my own for ten minutes. I was so excited I didn't know how those ten minutes passed. I don't even remember what I did.

One day, I took my family to the flying club and gave them a ride. They were thrilled. I had a yellow Pushpak. I used to fly loops over Navneet's house before we got married.

Between classes, I drove a tractor in the fields. During my holidays, I earned money for my flying lessons by driving tractors for people. It wasn't difficult at all because I enjoyed all the things I did thoroughly. I love farming; I still enjoy working on the land. But it was a physically stressful time, and it helped me prepare for the long hours that a pilot's life entails.

The Haryana government helped me complete my commercial pilot's lessons at the Kamal Aviation Club, in 1985. After graduating that year, I joined Indian Airlines as a co-pilot for the Boeing 737 fleet. In March 1986, I was sent for training. It was only in February 1996 that I took over as commander. I graduated to the Airbus recently, in March 1998.

So, on that chilly Christmas Eve morning, I thought my day would be like any other. First, I would be flying the New Delhi—Hyderabad morning flight. Then I would be flying IC 813 to Kathmandu and the return flight back. In my briefcase, I was carrying Navneet's pearls. I hoped I would have long enough in Delhi to go home for a while.

The day began well. I took off on schedule at 7 a.m. and was in New Delhi by 9 a.m. Fog delayed the flight to Kathmandu, which was scheduled for 11.15 a.m., by a couple of hours, and I could go home for a bit to leave my night kit and the pearls.

I called Navneet in Hyderabad when I got home.

'I reached a minute ago. Are you okay? Are the children all right?' The line was free of long-distance crackling.

'Everything's fine,' she said. 'Will you be in Hyderabad this evening?'

'I should be.'

'In case you have to stay back in Delhi, there's milk in the fridge, and also fruit juice.'

'Okay. I am leaving for Kathmandu now.'

I would remember these commonplace words during those eight days in hell. I wondered then what I would have said to her had I known the plane would be hijacked.

Chapter One

Kathmandu

24 December 1999

I took off on the A300 from Delhi at 1.45 p.m. and very soon we were flying over the mountains, glistening with snow, into Nepal. The descent went well and at 3.30 p.m. or so, we were at Kathmandu, inside the maelstrom that is Tribhuvan International Airport during tourist season. There wasn't much to do while the plane was refueled. I decided we needed extra fuel for our way back in case there was fog. This was to be a fateful decision. My co-pilot went to the Air Traffic Control (ATC) to get flight clearance.

The Kathmandu flight, IC 813, had been two and a half hours late and I got to Kathmandu very, very tired. My day had started early, and I had been in the cockpit for several hours. I felt I needed a short walk. Walking around the departure lounge, I met

Mr Lalchand, the station manager. He had got there a day or two ago and didn't seem very happy with the laid-back Kathmandu airport officials. I strolled around the security check area and noticed that it was all as casual as ever. There was a woman sitting in front of the baggage scanner knitting a sweater! I could have laughed at her, but for some reason I thought if anything hasn't happened, it is because God is on our side.

By now, all the Delhi passengers had gone through security check and were queuing outside the aircraft, so I had a minute to look around. Outside, I saw the airport wasn't even properly fenced off. All I could do was tell myself that if nothing had happened so far, nothing would happen in the future.

There were 178 passengers, and apart from my co-pilot Rajinder Kumar and flight engineer Anil Jaggia, there were eight cabin crew. We were a good crew, I think, well-knit and without fragile egos. The person I knew best was Mr Jaggia, with whom I had flown many times. He has always been a tower of strength. During the days ahead, I would always rely on his experience and advice. Of the cabin crew, I had also flown with Sapna Menon, one of the air hostesses, several times. The others I did not know so well but this would change. After the days of terror we spent together, we felt we had known one another for a long time. Anil Sharma was the senior flight purser. He was always known for being polite and diplomatic. Then there was Rajni Chandrashekhar. All my life, I'll remember how courageous she was during the hijacking. At Kandahar, she would come up to me and say, 'Captain, we are prepared for all eventualities.' Kalpana Mazumdar also seemed fearless, while Kobita Mukherjee laughed a lot and loudly, even in Kandahar. Sabita Khalko was very quiet and efficient, and was known for her stylish bindis. During the hijacking, her bindi was always in place. Tara Debnath was very quiet, unobtrusive and serious. Finally, there was young M.A. Satish, our junior flight purser.

Together, they were an efficient cabin crew, always willing to do anything, always well turned out, even right at the end of the hijacking crisis. I was proud of them.

About half an hour later, we were ready. In a couple of hours, I would be in New Delhi and then it was a question of meeting my wife at Hyderabad and flying off to Sharjah with the children.

All was well in the aircraft—I took off just after 4 p.m. and it was a smooth take-off. I had missed lunch and was very hungry. After taking off, I realized how late it was and decided to wait for tea. There wasn't much to do except set the course for Bhairahawa, a town on the India-Nepal border, a sort of marker for pilots, and later for Lucknow, the capital of Uttar Pradesh. It was still just another flight.

After fifteen minutes into the flight, we were cruising at 25,000 feet, flying at 0.78 Mach. I complained about the long delay in New Delhi—the plane had arrived from Calcutta very late.

'If the plane had arrived on time, we would have reached home much earlier,' I told Rajinder and Mr Jaggia. We entered Indian airspace. I relaxed and asked Anil Sharma for tea.

A few minutes later, Anil knocked on the cockpit door, and Mr Jaggia let him in. Anil served us and prepared to leave. I was leaning sideways, talking and laughing with Rajinder and Mr Jaggia when I saw someone enter the cockpit. He was wearing a red monkey cap that covered his whole face, except his eyes. He was also wearing dark glasses, a grey suit and a red tie. He was short and slight but with a bit of a belly. But these details I noticed later. What I noticed immediately were the pistol and the hand grenade he was carrying.

'What is all this?' I remember saying, almost to myself. That first moment when I saw him, I thought it was someone's idea of a joke. Then half a second later, I noticed Anil Sharma's ashen face and helpless expression. The man explained that he had a pistol and a grenade in his hand—I wasn't even listening, just trying to see if they were real weapons.

Something was wrong, terribly wrong. My plane had been hijacked, barely twenty minutes after I had taken off. It is difficult to explain how I felt just then. There were so many thoughts racing through in my mind. Foremost was concern for the passengers—they had to be saved. Then there was the sense of unreality that this was really happening. I remember the shock of being threatened by a gunman, the sensation of utter helplessness, amazement and pure fear. But it all happened so very quickly that there was no time to think.

We would later find out that this man was Ibrahim Athar, the brother of Maulana Masood Azhar, one of the three terrorists released on New Year's Eve in exchange for the passengers. The other hijackers called him Chief. He spoke slowly, with deliberate menace.

'*Koi harkat nehi hona chaiye.* (There should be no movement.)' Pointing to the hand grenade, he said, 'This is a bomb. I can blow up the airplane.'

He brandished the gun. 'This is loaded,' he said.

I knew the weapons weren't just toys. I had seen enough weapons during my days in the NCC to realize that these were real. But Chief wanted to reinforce the idea.

'*Isme goli hai* (There are bullets in it),' he said, pointing to the pistol. 'If I pull the pin, the grenade will go off.'

I was too numb to react. I stared at him. After what seemed an aeon, Chief spoke again. He seemed satisfied that he had driven home the point about the weapons. 'No one should speak without my permission. Do your job. Head west, head west.'

We were frozen with fear and said nothing. A moment later, Chief asked about air guards.

'We don't have any,' Rajinder said.

'There are no commandos on the plane either,' I said.

He wasn't convinced. 'I will search the plane. If I find any weapons on the plane, I won't spare any of you,' he threatened.

'Commercial planes don't have air guards,' Rajinder reiterated, but Chief still looked suspicious.

I was still hoping against hope that there was only one hijacker and that it would be possible somehow to resolve this problem easily. But just then, another man entered the cockpit. He was clad in black—black monkey cap, black T-shirt saying 'Kathmandu, Nepal', black jeans and tennis shoes. He too had a grenade in his left hand and a pistol in his right hand.

'Yes, Chief. Everything is under control,' he said. He was called Burger. I learnt later his real name was Sunny Ahmed Qazi, a member of the Harkat ul-Ansar from Karachi.

We were all shattered at the appearance of the second man. Rajinder slumped silently. When Mr Jaggia spoke to Burger, I could see he was badly frightened, '*Jo kahenge, hum karenge.* (We will do what you tell us to do.)' Burger did not respond.

'How much fuel do you have?' Chief asked me abruptly. I asked Mr Jaggia.

'Enough to go to New Delhi without problems,' he replied.

'No. Take this aircraft up to Lahore,' Chief said.

'We don't have enough fuel to go to Lahore,' I said.

'You have to take it to Lahore. Otherwise, this aircraft will be blown up.'

While talking amongst themselves, they seemed sure there was enough fuel. They seemed to have been briefed about fueling procedures, that we usually have some reserves, especially in winter, because of the fog.

A third hijacker entered the cockpit as they were talking. He was wearing checked trousers, a brown sleeveless jacket, a red T-shirt and a brown monkey cap. They called him Doctor (Shahid Akhtar Sayed, from Karachi). He had a knife in his hand, dangerously at the ready. The cockpit seemed full of people.

I turned to Chief.

'Do I have your permission to speak to the passengers?'

'Whatever you have to say has to be cleared by me.'

I told Chief I would ask the passengers to cooperate with the hijackers and tell them not to be afraid and to follow instructions. Chief agreed.

'Ladies and gentlemen, this is your captain, D. Sharan. Our plane has been hijacked. You must be patient and listen to the hijackers.'

Meanwhile, unseen by the hijackers I set my Air Traffic Control transponder to 7500 MHz, the hijacking code. This is an instrument that transmits the height, position and direction of the aircraft. When it is set at 7500 MHz, the ground control comes to know that the plane has been hijacked. In a matter of seconds, this information would be conveyed to all civil aviation authorities in India. They could then track the aircraft to see where it was going and at what height it was flying.

When I was setting my transponder code to 7500, Chief noticed. '*Aapne button daba diya kya*? (Have you pressed the emergency button?)' he asked. '*Aap hoshiyari mat dikhaiye.* (Don't try to be brave.) I'll shoot you if you do. You fly the plane. If you want to do anything else, ask for my permission.'

'I have to tell Varanasi ground control,' I said.

'Just fly the plane,' he said, unyielding.

I asked his permission to inform the ground control in Varanasi again and this time he agreed.

'We have been hijacked and are heading west,' I said to the ATC.

It was nearly 5 p.m., and we were over Lucknow when I saw two more hijackers, who also reported to Chief.

'Everything is under control,' they said.

One of them was Shankar (or Shakir, a Sindhi). He looked as brawny and tough as a commando. He too was clad in the regulation monkey cap, brown in his case, a grey T-shirt and jeans. The fifth hijacker was Bhola (Mistry Zahoor Ibrahim, from Karachi), short and wiry, dressed in a T-shirt and jeans. To me, he seemed the understudy, the willing learner beside the professionals. He was the worst behaved and was always rude to the passengers and crew. Flying over Lucknow, I changed my ATC on the ground from Varanasi to New Delhi. I reduced my flying speed by thirty per cent (from 320 knots to about 250 knots) so that people on the ground and the aviation authorities would have more time to prepare for the emergency. I was hoping the authorities would do something to rescue the passengers and us. After all, there was no certainty of landing at Lahore.

I could hear a great deal of noise coming from the cabin. I wondered what was happening there.

Ramesh Grover, a forty-four-year-old senior executive in an export firm, was amongst the first passengers to know that the plane was being hijacked. 'My seat number was 1B and if you look up, you can see the cockpit,' Grover said. 'The air hostess had just set the lunch tray on the table when I saw two masked guys. I thought it was some weird Indian Airlines Christmas ploy—it was Christmas Eve after all.' Then Grover heard one of them tell Anil Sharma to move back as the plane had been hijacked. 'I had taken off my shoes and was getting ready to have lunch. The hijacker flung the tray off the table. He didn't even allow me to put on my shoes. I was bundled over to the back of the plane. Like everyone else, I was blindfolded and sat with my head down.

'The piece of cloth wasn't large enough and it seemed to be coming off. One of the hijackers noticed.'

'*Patti khol diya tu ne*? (Have you taken off the blindfold?)' he asked menacingly and jabbed him in the back with his gun.

Grover replied the cloth wasn't large enough. The hijacker frisked him and gave him a replacement. Sitting blindfolded, Grover heard some pushing and shoving and the occasional crack of a slap.

Saibal Kar, a businessman, had a similar experience. 'We were about 15 to 20 minutes from Lucknow. It was like flying into a storm. I looked up from my laptop—I was in the second row—and I heard a loud noise, like something had fallen, and then I saw this guy wearing a monkey cap, carrying a gun. I figured, and rightly, that it was the guy sitting right behind me. I had turned around and seen him as we were taking off. He was tall, with long curly hair and a hooked nose,' he said. 'My laptop was open, I was writing out emails when he hit me on the side of my head with his pistol and said, "*Sar nichey karo. Ye bandh karo.* (Put your head down. Switch off your laptop.)" It's something so unexpected that it takes a few seconds to register, to work things out. You feel it's not happening. Then, you say to yourself, "Shit. We're being hijacked." Then, the fear takes over. You start living from moment to moment. There's nothing behind, there's nothing ahead. There's only the moment. Later, they bundled all of us business class passengers to the back of the plane. I remember the frenzy...there they were, the hijackers, running up and down, waving their pistols or knives, hitting people, screaming, shouting.'

For Sanjeev Sharma, another passenger, the first emotion was disbelief. 'The hijacking was so sudden. This man was sitting right in front of me and suddenly, he's coming out of the toilet, waving his gun. "Shit, this is it," I thought. "This is a hijacking." We were almost immediately sure they were Kashmiris or Pakistanis. I thought they were taking revenge for the Pakistani naval reconnaissance aircraft shot down in the Sir Creek area by the Air Force.'

Geeta Baisala, wife of the personal assistant to the Indian ambassador in Kathmandu, was flying back to New Delhi with her three children.

'It started with some shouting which I ignored. I continued eating. I thought people were quarrelling. When it didn't stop, I turned around to see what was happening. Just then, I saw masked men running down the aisles, waving their knives and pistols saying "No one move. We have hijacked the plane." I was worried about my children. Prashant is five and Akansha is three—they were sitting behind me, while I was holding Kirti.'

One of the passengers said that he noticed a young man in a hood—only his eyes and nose were visible—get up with a pistol and grenade in his hand. When no one seemed to take notice at first, he thought it was a mock exercise till the captain's message. The hijackers took this passenger to be a commando and searched him three times, a pistol at his temple. They only found his Election Commission identity card, and that made them even more suspicious. He kept a diary of these days, jotting down things on scraps of paper, and even his trousers and boarding card.

More orders rang out. Everyone had to put their heads down. 'The uncles are very angry. They are shouting at us. Put your heads down,' Mrs Baisala told Prashant and Akansha. The children obeyed.

'There were two men who stood near the curtain that separates the executive class from the economy class. Two others were standing at the rear end. They told us not to look up and to raise our hands if we wanted something,' she said. They promised that no one would be harmed if the passengers listened to them. Later, the men were moved to the back and the women brought up to the front.

'The women were told to cover their heads. I did not cover my eyes. They didn't say anything to me about it. Only later I realized all the other women had completely veiled themselves,' Mrs Baisala said. But she discovered that the hijackers, especially Burger, were kind to her children. When Akansha started crying, they brought her sweets. They also told the adults to save the soft drinks and the milk for the children.

Seema Jain found herself and her daughters, aged seven and four, separated from her husband Amit. The hijackers moved him to a seat four rows behind theirs.

'I knew he was there...but it is strange to be in a situation where the person you wish to speak to is sitting within hearing distance, but you are not permitted to speak to him. Though you can't speak or see, you can still hear.'

Ashok Kathuria almost missed the hijacking. 'I was in the loo when the whole thing happened. By the time I came out, they had taken over the plane. Then Shankar prodded me and told me to sit somewhere. I did.'

Navneet Sharan was spending the day with friends in Hyderabad. She kept expecting her husband back in the late afternoon and decided to make some *pulao* for him and their friends.

At 5.40 p.m., the phone rang. Harminder Singh of Indian Airlines was calling from New Delhi. She didn't notice the edge of panic in his normally cheerful voice and thought he was calling to say Captain Sharan's flight was delayed.

'I won't listen to anything. Make sure Captain Sharan is here. We're leaving for Sharjah,' she told Singh.

'That's not the reason why I am calling,' he replied quietly.

'How did you know I am here? Where are you? Are you in Hyderabad?' she asked.

'I am in New Delhi,' he sounded desperate. 'Captain Sharan's aircraft has been hijacked. He has asked you to return home.' He was trying to reassure her.

'Did you actually speak to him?' she asked, fearing the worst.

'Yes. I'll call you back.'

The phone was soon ringing again.

'Bhabiji, you're coming back to Delhi?' Singh said.

'Tell me truthfully. Is it just a hijack?'

'Yes, yes. He's alive!'

A little later, the station manager of Hyderabad airport called. 'Madam, we have decided for you. How do we recognize you?' he asked.

'I'll be with my two beautiful daughters,' Navneet replied. She still felt that she hadn't been told the whole truth and tried once more to find out.

'What happened?'

'Don't you know?'

'I want you to tell me.'

'Captain Sharan's plane has been hijacked.'

She rang off. 'My daughters were crying. There were tears in my eyes when I set off... I only remembered the advice I had been given by Captain Sharan's friend, U.S. Datta, whose house we had been staying at in Hyderabad. "Don't get too emotional and tell the press something that would affect Captain Sharan." People were calling out to me at the airport, but I couldn't answer.'

Sitting in the Movement Control Room, she looked up at the board listing the flights for the day. Captain Sharan had flown the first Indian Airlines flight of the day: Hyderabad–Delhi.

'Whatever happens, please let me know,' she told the air hostesses, who were more attentive than usual.

As she sat on the plane, she realized that anything could happen to him and was deeply thankful for the eleven years they had spent together. 'I must take care of the children, I thought, and told them "Papa will be back for dinner." I must reassure them, I said to myself.'

Just then, the air hostess came over. 'Captain Sharan has landed in Amritsar.'

In all this confusion, there was one certainty: we were getting closer and closer to New Delhi. I told New Delhi ATC about the 'excess baggage' on the flight—the hijackers and the arms and ammunition they were carrying. We were still conversing on radio telephone, but the control tower gave me an exclusive frequency so that the conversations would be uninterrupted and therefore easier.

I spoke to Rajinder and Mr Jaggia, and then to Chief. 'Tell us what to do and we will do it, but please don't harm the passengers.'

I realized I had to pull myself together and think calmly. I had a plane to fly; I had my passengers to think of. I needed to size up the hijackers—I had to know what they were about. Who were they? I didn't know anything beyond their comic-book names. Where were they from? Pakistan, probably. Maybe even Pakistan-occupied Kashmir. Chief spoke Urdu, the others Urdu and Hindi. All of them were armed: Chief, Burger and Bhola were carrying pistols and hand grenades, one in each hand; Doctor had a knife, and Shankar, a grenade. I knew we couldn't overpower the hijackers; it was a risk we couldn't take. We would be brave but tactful and diplomatic. We would follow every instruction; we would do everything they asked us to, but we would have to get the passengers back home safely. Chief's mantra was 'West, west, fly west.' He said if we made any suspicious movements, he would blow up the plane right there: one look at him and I knew he meant every word he said. They were fanatics, death-or-glory men.

We could hear the radio transmissions of Victor-Victor-Alpha, Prime Minister Atal Behari Vajpayee's plane.

'Victor-Victor-Alpha? Huh!' Chief said. He knew it was the prime minister's plane. He turned to technicalities again. 'We have to fly for five hours,' he said.

'I have fuel for three hours. I have to take permission to bypass New Delhi.'

I was on the line to New Delhi. I wanted permission to land in Lahore, but they said they couldn't get permission. For the hijackers, Lahore was crucial.

'Even if they don't permit, you'll have to keep on trying,' Chief said.

Captain Devi Sharan was trying. At 11.34 a.m. Greenwich Mean Time—all aircraft fly on GMT—or 5.04 p.m. Indian Standard Time, he asked New Delhi ATC for Lahore weather. Four minutes later he had received the details.

As the plane crossed Jalalabad, he called CENTOP—the Central Operations Centre of Indian Airlines—in New Delhi.

The tape transcript of Frequency 124.2 MHz indicates the growing alarm in the cockpit, and the slow, almost guarded reactions on the ground. This was perhaps natural; everyone had been taken by surprise and was unsure of what to do.

At 5.11 p.m. IST, Captain Sharan was on the line to New Delhi and, over the next two hours, he relayed the demands of the hijackers.

'They are telling us to head for Lahore. Can you take permission from Lahore to land?'

The reply: 'Roger, sir, stand by.'

He was fifty-eight miles short of Sikandrabad, heading for Lahore.

At 5.18 p.m., he was still asking for permission to land at Lahore. He was told they were coordinating.

At 5.24 p.m., Captain Sharan was told: 'Lahore refused to accept the flight.'

But the hijackers were insistent.

'They are insisting. They are saying the aircraft will go there and nowhere else.'

'Number of Hotel-India-Juliet?' asked Delhi. It was a coded enquiry to find out how many hijackers were on board—HIJ being the first three letters of the word.

'About five,' the Captain replied. 'They have got everything on board—everybody has got a pistol or a revolver.'

'Roger. Thank you.'

'Dynamite. They have grenades.'

It was 5.27 p.m. IC 849 was nearby and the captain, R.N. Singh, who was an old associate of Captain Sharan came on the line. He was the general manager (operations) in New Delhi.

'RN here. What is the problem?'

'We have been hijacked, sir. About five people on board and they have everything—grenades, pistols.' Captain Singh tried to be reassuring.

'Oh, no problem. Be cool and just follow what they say and confirm they boarded at Kathmandu.'

'Affirm, sir.'

'They want to go where? To Lahore?'

'Affirm, sir.'

'Okay. Anyway, just be cool and just do what they say and everything will be all right.'

But their troubles were just beginning.

At 5.36 p.m., Captain Sharan was informed that Lahore had not permitted the landing. Enraged, the hijackers started threatening violence.

'They want to go to Lahore only... They are saying that if you try to act tough, they will blow up the plane. They have everything on board,' Captain Sharan warned. He asked for permission to contact Lahore directly.

At 5.51 p.m., Captain Sharan informed New Delhi: 'Lahore is not accepting us. Runway is blocked...'

The hijackers were adamant. It would have to be Lahore.

'They are insisting I try to land on the blocked runway. That is their final decision,' the Captain said, at 5.55 p.m. Three minutes later, he said the plane was ninety-seven miles from Lahore and if he wasn't allowed to land, the hijackers would kill one passenger. For perhaps the first time, the IC 814 crew and the ground staff realized the full extent of fanatical intensity of the hijackers.

Captain Sharan again repeated the threat at 5.57 p.m. 'We are eighty-one miles now [from Lahore]... They want us to land only in Lahore. Otherwise, they will kill us one by one.'

He had fuel for only an hour, he said. He had a little more than that. It was 6 p.m.

The hijackers huddled around him as Captain Sharan cried to contact Lahore once more.

But Lahore did not want IC 814. 'Don't enter our airspace,' said the ground control officer. 'Otherwise, there will be serious consequences.'

Sharan had to contact New Delhi ATC again.

'Sir, Pakistan is not letting us enter their airspace now. You tell us what to do... Can we proceed overhead to Lahore or proceed to Amritsar?'

'You can proceed to Amritsar from present position', was the reply.

'We will proceed but they are not letting us land.'

At 6.06 p.m., New Delhi confirmed that Lahore was impossible.

'Lahore is not available...they are not permitting any other aircraft, not even their own aircraft.'

A minute later, Captain Sharan heard the same voice repeating the same dire message.

'Lahore is not permitting PIA (Pakistan International Airlines) aircraft also for landing and departure.'

IC 814 was running out of time. In a little while, it would be running out of fuel.

Chapter Two

Amritsar

24 December 1999

From the tapes of the conversations between the ATC at Raja Sansi Airport, Amritsar, and Captain Sharan, one can sense the tension, the panic in the cockpit and the inability of the officials to act quickly.

It was now 12.34 p.m. GMT (6.04 p.m. IST) and Captain Sharan was calling Amritsar on the Very High Frequency channel.

'Maintaining flight level 260—forty-one miles short of AAR. Will be holding over VIAR. We have only one hour's fuel and Lahore is not letting us enter their airspace,' he said. AAR is Alpha Alpha Romeo, a Very High Frequency code for Amritsar. VIAR is the code for Amritsar airport. For pilots, the country is divided into four zones—Delhi, Mumbai, Calcutta and Chennai. The code for Delhi is VI and Amritsar, of course, is AR.

A minute later, the Captain was repeating the same message.

'Maintaining flight level 260—thirty-eight miles short of you. OPLA [Lahore] is not letting us enter their airspace.'

At 6.13 p.m. IST, Captain Sharan was very close to Amritsar airport.

'Request your intentions,' said Amritsar ATC.

'They want to go to Lahore as we have been hijacked,' the Captain replied. 'We have only forty minutes' fuel. Lahore is not letting us land as their runway is blocked. We cannot land there. They [the hijackers] say we have to land even if runway is blocked.'

It was now 6.18 p.m. IST, and Captain Sharan was desperate. 'They are insisting we go to Lahore and they are not allowing us to land on Indian soil.'

A minute later, Amritsar said: 'We are ready to extend all facilities. Request your intentions.'

'Situation is serious on board. Request authorities to get landing permission for Lahore...' replied Captain Sharan.

At 6.21 p.m., Sharan's message conveys the tension in the cabin. 'They must land in Lahore. Otherwise, they are ready to crash.'

Two minutes later, he was shouting out in panic. 'They will start shooting. They have already selected ten passengers.'

At 6.32 p.m.: 'We are negotiating through Delhi area with Lahore. Unfortunately, Lahore runway is blocked. That is why they are not in a position to accept any aircraft.'

At 6.34 p.m., the A300 had fuel for only thirty minutes. Captain Sharan was still standing by for further instructions.

At 6.42 p.m., the plane was still circling over Amritsar and had clearance for Halwara, an Indian Air Force base.

'We are now in [an] emergency [situation]. We have only twenty-five minutes' fuel,' the Captain reported. Halwara, he was told, was approximately a hundred and fifty kilometres away.

Inside the cockpit, the flight crew pleaded with the hijackers.

'The plane is running out of fuel. Please let us land at Amritsar. Otherwise, the plane will crash,' I begged Chief.

But he had decided. 'We won't land in Amritsar. Let the plane run out of fuel and crash.'

I was so overcome with desperation that I bent down and touched his feet. So did Rajinder and Mr Jaggia. All of us said the same thing. 'Please let us land in Amritsar.' I couldn't see his eyes. But he did seem to relent and went back into the cabin to speak with the other hijackers.

When he came back a few moments later, he said, 'I want the plane refueled in three minutes.'

'Okay, I promise. We'll start refueling in three minutes.' That suited us fine. We didn't want to leave Indian air space. We had clearance from Halwara.

'No,' said Chief. 'Not Halwara. It must be Amritsar.'

At 6.44 p.m., the plane was getting ready to land at Amritsar. Captain Sharan reported their requirements to Amritsar ATC.

'We are descending now. They are going to park on the runway itself... Fuel tanker. Send the fuel tanker, they have everything...revolvers, AK-47s, grenades... They want refueling immediately.' He was also unhappy about the functioning of one of the engines and wanted a repair job done.

He was told that the refueling had been arranged and that there was no other vehicle on the runway except the bowser.

As we landed, I was thinking of my various options. Could I immobilize the plane in some way—by taking it off the runway, into the fields? I realized I couldn't do it.

Considering the number of arms the hijackers had and their do-or-die attitude, it would be dangerous for the passengers. My primary duty was to save the passengers, not endanger their lives by taking the plane off the runway. Also, airline policy does not allow such an act: it requires the pilot to follow the instructions of the hijackers.

At 7.00 p.m., the plane landed. The ground control wanted the plane shifted and asked Captain Sharan to put one of the hijackers on the line.

'Woh aapse bat nahi karna chahte (They don't want to speak to you),' the Captain replied. 'Send the bowser immediately. They want fuel.'

Inside the A300 cockpit, Chief was standing warily right behind the Captain's seat.

'Stop, stop,' he shouted. He seemed to think an Airbus stopped like a car, that it could come to a stop as soon as it landed. When the plane finally stopped, Chief barked out further orders.

'Keep the engines running and keep turning the aircraft around.'

The plane had to be kept moving up and down the runway. The pilots kept turning the plane at 180 degrees, sometimes to the east, sometimes to the west. There was a road running parallel to the runway, and whenever a jeep or a motorcycle sped by, the hijackers would become nervous. 'The commandos are coming. I know they are coming. Move, move, move,' Chief kept reiterating.

By 7.05 p.m., Captain Sharan was again pleading with the Amritsar ATC. Both engines were shut down. Captain Sharan had switched off Engine 2 at 7.02 p.m. and Engine 1 a minute later.

'Please send it [the bowser] fast. We have only five minutes.'

'Roger, sir.'

'Please send within five minutes.'

'Affirmative, sir. We have already informed Indian Oil. They should be on the way. Because this is not the usual time of landing, Indian Oil was closed. We have alerted them.'

'Please send it fast. Otherwise, one of us will be shot.'

'Immediately, sir. As soon as they will come, they will immediately be on site.'

It was now 7.07 p.m. The tension level in the cockpit was rising palpably every moment. The hijackers wanted their fuel immediately. And there was no sign yet of the bowser. In the aircraft, Burger was getting vicious. 'Why don't you have any fuel?' he raged. 'We'll cut a few throats. We'll kill a few people and then, there will be fuel.'

Chief was calmer. 'Don't do anything now. Wait a little,' he advised.

Sharan was on the RT (radio telephone set). 'They are saying: "*Agar kisine ustadi dikhane ki koshish ki, sub ko bhoon ke rakh denge*! (If someone tries to be too clever, we will kill everyone!)" They have grenades in their hands and revolvers and AK-47s.'

'No *ustadi.* Only slight delay because the fueling station was closed. We have already acted. Your aircraft will be refueled,' replied the ground controller.

But at 7.11 p.m.' Captain Sharan was still calling for the bowser. And the ground controller was still stalling.

'Send the bowser fast. Please, only two minutes left,' the Captain pleaded.

'Roger, sending,' the ground controller replied.

'They want just two people on the bowser.'

'Roger.'

Half a minute later, Captain Sharan was back on the RT. 'Please send it fast. Send it fast. Send it fast. Now guns are pointed at our heads.'

'Affirmative, sir! We are sending it very fast.'

'Everybody will be shot. Another three to five minutes. Kindly please come.'

At 7.14 p.m., at the orders of the hijackers, Captain Sharan started Engine 2. He had already started Engine 1, and now began turning the aircraft around again. The hijackers did not want the engines to be shut down. They wanted to be able to escape instantly in case there was any sign of a rescue operation. The ATC was still saying that the bowser was on its way.

After talking amongst themselves, Chief and Burger came back to me.

'We need petrol, more petrol,' Chief said. 'How much fuel do you have? Can you go to Lahore with what you have?'

'No, we can't,' I said. 'Certainly not.'

The orders rang out. 'Take the plane to Lahore. If you can't, crash the plane. We don't really care.'

'What good will that do?' I asked.

I tried to calculate how much fuel we had. How many tons? I realized we had about three tons, just enough to reach Lahore.

'If the plane crashes, you'll get some money. Insurance. If I shoot you, you won't get that,' Chief said. 'I want the plane to crash here, right on the runway.'

Again, Burger and the others began threatening to kill the passengers.

But Chief quietened them. '*Abhi nahin.*'

I was trying to pacify them. 'The bowser will come immediately. See, it's coming.'

But there was no bowser.

It was now 7.17 p.m. The Captain was still trying to get the bowser.

'Send the bowser fast. Send the bowser fast. They do not have patience. They are going to... A grenade will burst here.'

'The bowser is starting right now. It has started. It is reaching there.'

'Guns are on our shoulders. Please send the bowser fast.'

'It is coming immediately.'

'What is immediately? Where is it?'

'Okay. Let's see. *Kahan par hain*? *Yaar, waha par hain nahi*? (Where is it? Friend, it's not there?).'

'We're moving ahead. Send the bowser now.'

'Affirmative, sir. Sending the bowser.'

'Where is the bowser? Where is the bowser? Yaar, yaar. He has started killing the passengers. Why don't you understand our problem... He has already killed a passenger now.'

In the cabin, I suspected, the passengers were being terrorized. I learnt later that they were all made to sit with their heads down, blindfolded. Seven men had been brought to the executive class and tied up. Ripin Katyal and Satnam Singh had been stabbed. Everyone was petrified that they would be killed any moment.

At 7.27 p.m., there was a state of complete panic in the cockpit. We had already spent half an hour on the tarmac. 'Now where is the bowser?' I asked.

The ATC replied: 'It has started moving. You will be able to see the light.'

'Where is it?' I asked.

At 7.29 p.m., I again pleaded for the bowser. 'Guns are on our heads, and they are going to kill anybody now. Anybody, any time.'

They replied: '*Theek hain. Note kar liyaa. Abhi dekhiye wo pahuchne wallen hain. Light aap ko nazar aa rahee hogee shayad.* (Okay. I have noted it down. The bowser should have reached by now. You may be in a position to see the light.)'

I was feeling very afraid and abandoned. Wasn't anyone listening to me? Wasn't anyone coming to save us?

In the cabin, the hijackers had already gone berserk.

Burger walked into the cabin.

'Chief, we have killed four people.'

I was shocked. I asked Mr Jaggia to go to the cabin and check things out. When he got up, Burger dragged him into the executive class. He saw two people bleeding profusely, their throats slit. There was blood on the floor.

Doctor was there, knife in hand.

'*Tumhe bhi marte hain* (It will be your turn),' he said, and wiped his knife on Mr Jaggia's shirt. I saw the bloodstains when he came back and sat down. He looked as if he was about to break down.

'Mr Jaggia, what have they done?'

'They have killed people.' He was shaking.

At 7.30 p.m., I had switched off Engine 2 again. There was little I could do but continue calling for the bowser.

'Look, it is to your east.'

'Which side are you talking about, friend?' I said tiredly.

The bowser was coming up. It drove down a side lane towards the aircraft.

'Is it on my left, or right?' the Captain asked, in Hindi.

'It is on your right,' was the reply.

'My right.'

'No, no, sorry. Left side. You should be able to see the vehicle moving up.'

'Tell me where.'

'It's reached the runway. You must have spotted it.'

'Okay, okay,' the Captain sounded relieved. It was 7.31 p.m.

'Can you see the lights?'

'Yes. We are getting ready for refueling. We are shutting down the engines now.'

From the ground control came the advice: 'Speak to the hijackers and ask them to cool down.'

'They are cool. They have cooled down. They say they want to go from here. That is all. I have shut down the engine. Send the bowser fast.'

'Do they understand English or not? Do they speak in English? Which language do they speak?'

The Captain was asked to keep turning the plane. 'We are starting Engine 1 and heading south. Bring the bowser in front of us. They do not want any kind of car or anything behind the bowser,' he reported.

At 7.35 p.m., the Captain was still waiting for the refueling operations to begin.

'Send the bowser. Why is the bowser lying on the runway side?'

The next message, a moment later, sounded completely panic-stricken.

'He is going to start shooting us now. Shooting us. You have not sent the bowser. Do not delay. Please come. He is going to kill us now.'

At 7.38 p.m., again: 'Why aren't you sending the bowser? They have already killed one person.'

The reply: 'Have you stopped the aircraft? The bowser said the aircraft is moving.'

'Aircraft is not moving. Aircraft is standing.'

A minute later: 'They have already killed one person. A second person has now been killed.'

At 7.43 p.m., Captain Sharan still could not see the bowser. There was now a note of complete weariness. He had been calling for a bowser for nearly an hour.

'They are going to kill everybody. Four persons have already been killed.'

At 7.46 p.m., he tried one last time. 'Where is the bowser, yaar?'

'It is on the way, sir.'

'What do you mean "It is on the way." You know they have killed passengers. They want to see the bowser first.'

Inside the cockpit, the pressure was almost unbearable. I was calling and calling but there was no response. There was no bowser. While all this was going on, the hijackers were increasingly getting more jittery and more murderous.

'Take off or we'll kill you,' Burger said. 'Take off and crash the plane.'

After a few minutes, Chief ordered: '*Aur char log ko maro.* (Kill another four people.) I am beginning a countdown. If you don't take off, we'll kill everyone.'

And then Chief began: 'Thirty, twenty-nine, twenty-eight...'

The gun was at Mr Jaggia's head. When he reached sixteen, I pulled back my chair and turned towards Chief.

'Please stop,' I requested him and touched his feet. He pointed his gun at me.

'Don't hurt him. He has little children,' Mr Jaggia said.

But the countdown was starting again.

'Fifteen, fourteen.' He was counting a little slowly. I remember his voice, soft and deliberate.

In desperation, Mr Jaggia put his hand over Chief's mouth, pushing him off balance.

Chief slapped his hand away and hit him.

'*Yeh bahut bolta hain* (He talks too much),' he said. He continued counting. 'Eight, seven, six...'

We had spotted the bowser. It was nearing the aircraft but was still five hundred feet away.

When they were down to 'two' and about to shoot Mr Jaggia and me, I began preparing for take-off. I had no choice. I was sorely disappointed that my aircraft could not be stopped. We were going to Lahore. There was no option left. Mr Jaggia had told me about what had happened in the cabin and Chief was ordering the others to cut four more throats... We were on the tarmac for forty-nine minutes and both engines had remained switched off for eleven minutes, enough time, I think, for a commando operation.

But nothing happened, there was no rescue effort, and we were forced to fly again. As I switched on the engines and took off, I felt terrible. I had never felt worse in my life. This was our chance to stop the hijackers. And we had blown it. Now I didn't know where we would go and how many of us would come out alive.

At 7.49 p.m., Captain Sharan said, 'We are taking off.'

The transcript, signed by the airport director, Amritsar, on 23 January 2000, states that the radio operators could hear people crying on the aircraft. Captain Sharan would send a few messages over the next four minutes:

'We are taking off. We are all dying now. No bowser... We are heading towards Lahore. IC 814 has no fuel... You inform Lahore about this. We have no fuel. They have already killed four passengers. It is confirmed. You did not understand... They only wanted to refuel.'

It had been a long wait for the bowser that never came. In the cabin, the hijackers, apprehending a commando operation, had pulled out their knives soon after the plane landed.

Seema Jain described those moments of terror. 'I heard the terrorists warn a man [Ripin Katyal] three times. He was apparently trying to raise his head and find out what they were up to. I prayed that God would somehow make my husband sit still on his seat. I knew it was impossible to keep still for so many hours. But I prayed he would not raise his head. I did not hear the hijackers warn my husband. He must have obeyed their orders.

'I saw my husband sitting with his head between his knees when I was getting back from the toilet. I looked at him for as long as I could. It was for only a few seconds...'

The passengers couldn't just go to the toilet when they needed to. The hijackers would call out the seat numbers. In those fourteen hours, Seema would go three times. They were blindfolded almost throughout, except when they were served food. They knew they were landing somewhere but they didn't know where.

'We had no idea about what was happening. Every time the plane landed; I would pray for our release. And then, the plane would take off again. Late in the evening, I wanted some milk for the children. I raised my hand quietly and hoped. One of the hijackers brought me a glass of milk. It was cold but I didn't complain,' remembers Geeta Baisala.

Like the Jains, the Vermas were also returning from a vacation in Kathmandu. Indu Verma and her two children were also separated from her husband.

'I kept my daughter [Urvi, one and a half years old] with myself and sent my five-year-old son Shaurya to be with my husband. It was easier to look after my daughter.'

Since the plane had not been refueled and their plans foiled, the hijackers started acting against those who 'disobeyed' them. Katyal had raised his head—he would have to answer for it. For Satnam Singh, who was made to sit next to Katyal and knifed by the hijackers, those moments were terrifying.

'They were very tense. They didn't want anyone to look up. They were shouting at each other to start with. And when the request for refueling was refused, they went berserk.

'They picked out seven or eight passengers and took them to the executive class cabin. Ripin Katyal and I were among them. They chose us probably because we were well-built and they thought we were the ones who would fight back.' The others included Daman Soni, Chander Chabbra and a European.

'I think they warned the authorities they would kill passengers if the plane wasn't refueled. Incensed by the delay, the hijackers acted. Doctor had a knife with a smallish blade he had sneaked in.

'It was all very sudden. Doctor was standing near me and stabbed me four times just under my chin, twice on my cheeks and once in my neck. I fell but I saw them catch hold of Ripin Katyal and stab him in the neck... That's when I fainted.'

The others were beaten up—the cabin floor was wet with blood.

Satnam Singh was relatively lucky. One of the passengers, Dr Anita Joshi, gave him two painkillers. Efforts to help Katyal, who was sitting next to Singh, failed. He was wounded in the throat and neck, and bleeding profusely. He couldn't swallow water or pain killers. They threw a blanket over Katyal, but by the time the passengers were released at Dubai, he had died of excessive bleeding. Later, Doctor said he had been asking Katyal to keep quiet for a while, but he hadn't listened. 'Now,' he said 'he'll keep quiet.'

Sharan had risked the hijacker's wrath much earlier to inform aviation authorities of the hijacking. This was when IC 814 was flying west, over Uttar Pradesh and towards New Delhi and subsequently, Lahore, but Varanasi ATC informed Delhi ATC only at 4.52 p.m. about the hijacking on a landline. Minutes later, at 4.56 p.m., the earlier report was confirmed. After sending the coded message on his transponder, Captain made radio contact, officially informing the ATC about the armed hijackers and their destination: Lahore. It was now up to the Crisis Management Group (CMG) headed by cabinet secretary Prabhat Kumar to deal with the crisis. Would the wheels of government move quickly on a freezing afternoon on Christmas

Eve? The early warning was in vain, it seemed. There was some delay early on: Delhi airport probably didn't have the recent telephone numbers of CMG officials. Prime Minister Atal Behari Vajpayee (wishing him 'happy seventy-fifth birthday' the next day would be a travesty!) was flying back from Bihar along with the civil aviation minister, Sharad Yadav, after a public meeting, but neither was informed immediately. He was only informed at 5.20 p.m., after he landed. Fifteen minutes later, after reaching his Race Course Road residence, he called a cabinet meeting. Soon after this, Yadav made an official statement where he called Pakistan's role in the hijacking 'suspicious'. At 6 p.m., the CMG officials—the cabinet secretary, principal secretary to the prime minister Brajesh Mishra, the National Security Guard chief Nikhil Kumar, the home secretary Kamal Pande, the foreign secretary Lalit Mansingh and the intelligence agency chiefs, A.S. Dulat of Research and Analysis Wing (RAW) and Shyamal Dutta of the Intelligence Bureau (IB)—gathered at Rajiv Gandhi Bhavan. The meeting started an hour late.

The hijackers had taken India by surprise. At the Rajiv Gandhi Bhawan, the entire establishment groped for answers, for solutions; they found none.

'No one knew what to do. We were simply improvising,' said Lalit Mansingh, then foreign secretary. He hadn't known there was a CMG, he wasn't even aware he was a member.

Signs of confusion, signs of an unprepared government trying to find answers, were everywhere. 'As I entered, I saw a blackboard with a lot of names on it. It said: "Salman Haidar, foreign secretary."And Salman Haidar was not my predecessor. He was my predecessor's predecessor. This was just one example of how dysfunctional it all was.' Nor was the Crisis Management Group "managing" anything. 'It was a misnomer. It was more a crisis monitoring group. It was not clear what our powers were. There were different meetings happening in different places.'

The Cabinet Committee on Security (CCS) would meet later. 'Brajesh Mishra, the National Security Advisor, besides being principal secretary to the prime minister, was at our meeting. He would be with members of the CCS, headed by Prime Minister Vajpayee. On the large TV screen, we saw the plane's flight path. The events of Amritsar were in full view, but our discussions were not cogent. Nobody took a decision. There were people on their cell phones. They were saying how many policemen there were at the airport. There was a lot of exchange of information. There were no decisions.'

They were there all night, most of India's leading officials. Not part of the CMG were the Army, Navy and Air Force chiefs. 'When the plane took off, I realized it was my job as well,' said Mansingh. 'No decision to deny fuel was taken, there had been no "wargaming" on this, there were "no standard operating procedures." The NSG didn't even take off for Amritsar; they were waiting for a psychologist,' he said, regretfully.

With Sharan's plane in the air, it was time to reach out to other countries. 'I asked for a list of passengers,' said Mansingh. There was an American on board. 'I called Dick (Richard) Celeste, the US Ambassador to India. "Dick, we have a problem. One of your guys is on the plane." He promised to speak with the Pakistanis and the UAE officials. It helped as the US State Department got into the act. In New Delhi, Celeste spoke with the Pakistan high commissioner to India, and I spoke with the Swiss and Belgian ambassadors, the British high commissioner, and also, with G. Parthasarathy, then our high commissioner to Islamabad, and K.C. Singh, our ambassador to the UAE.'

As important as the CMG in this present crisis was, its tactical wing, its central committee (CC), was headed by the director-general, civil aviation, H.S. Khola. The others in the CC include members of the Airports Authority and the Bureau of Civil Aviation Security. Their role involves informing all airports where the hijacked plane can land. Each airport has an Aerodrome Committee, usually headed by a district magistrate or commissioner. The Hijacking Contingency Plan, 1987, revised in August 1995, states that the committee must 'engage the hijackers,' which means persuading them to surrender or at least, slowing them down to allow the commandos time to storm the aircraft. The district magistrate or commissioner is supposed to be aided by the senior superintendent of police (SSP), the airport manager and a member of the IB. Their role is to find out who the hijackers are and what they want.

In Chandigarh, Sarabjeet Singh, director-general of police, Punjab, first heard of the hijacking on television. He ordered his policemen in Amritsar to reach Raja Sansi Airport. And they did, before the flight landed. There were enough brass hats at the airport. There was an inspector-general of police, J.P. Birdi. Having been alerted, Narinderjit Singh, district magistrate of Amritsar, had reached the airport and met the airport director, Vijay Mulekar, who was already monitoring the developments along with the senior airport officer, Tarlok Singh. Two more senior policemen—deputy inspector-general, Jasminder Singh, and senior superintendent of police, P.P.S. Sandhu—arrived later, as did Punjab Police commandos.

The entire Aerodrome Committee sat inside the ATC tower at 7.00 p.m. as Captain Sharan landed the A300. It was already two hours and eight minutes since the authorities in New Delhi had been informed about the hijacking and about forty-five minutes since it was obvious that Captain Sharan was trying to land at Amritsar. Now, everyone thought, the hijackers' game was up; nothing would go wrong. The committee had orders from

New Delhi, crisp and terse: the aircraft would not be refueled. It was to be delayed for as long as possible. The delay would allow the National Security Guard (NSG) the time it needed. In an hour or so, it seemed, the passengers would be freed, and the hijackers captured or dead.

Captain Sharan's A300 was still on the tarmac, his appeals for the bowser were being dealt with when the telephone rang in the Amritsar ATC. The caller stated that he was J. Lal of the ministry of home affairs, calling from his North Block office in New Delhi. He had new orders: refuel the aircraft and allow it to leave. There was further confusion in the ATC but Mr Lal's orders were not carried out. For, after cursory checking, it was clear that there was no J. Lal in the home ministry and the call came from sources which could not be traced.

Delay the refueling the Aerodrome Committee did, in their tardiness in responding to the repeated requests from Captain Sharan. Beyond that, the facts aren't clear. Was the Aerodrome Committee asked to immobilize the aircraft? Or was it asked to merely delay the refueling? 'Immobilize,' says the officials in New Delhi who were monitoring the hijacking, perhaps by shooting the tyres off. 'Delay,' says the officials of the Aerodrome Committee in Amritsar. They did do so, until they could hear terror from the aircraft. The hijackers had blood on their knives. As K.P.S. Gill, once India's most famous policeman, and a man who foiled two hijackings, later said, 'Sending and receiving messages through Chandigarh only delayed and confused the process. [The communication] should have been New Delhi–Amritsar and Amritsar–New Delhi.'

Communication was further complicated by the fact that there were many different channels of communication. At 7.10 p.m., the cabinet secretary, Prabhat Kumar, spoke to SSP Sandhu, telling him to delay the refueling and ensure the plane didn't take off. Shortly afterwards, principal secretary to the prime minister, Brajesh Mishra reiterated to DIG Jasminder Singh that every effort should be made to ensure the plane didn't take off.

Gill states that there was 'total lack of coordination between New Delhi, Chandigarh and Amritsar. Different officers were separately receiving instructions from New Delhi and Chandigarh, and there was no coordination of this information with the officers negotiating with the hijackers.'

As Gill says: 'It is already clear that no one person was in charge at the Amritsar ATC. The cabinet secretary was instructing the SSP, the prime minister's principal secretary was speaking to the DIG, and the state DGP to the IG. The man talking to the pilot was Vijay Mulekar.' One reason for the confusion was the lack of STD lines at the ATC's office so that mobile phones belonging to the police had to be used for communication.

There was a half-baked effort to block the A300 by parking a fuel truck right in front of the plane. It was a decent enough idea, but poorly executed. The driver was perhaps too eager. He went too quickly and braked too suddenly, arousing more suspicions among the jittery hijackers. They were on enemy territory, and they wanted Captain Sharan to fly off.

Was delaying sending the bowser such a great idea? Gill believes that if the Indian Oil bowser had reached the plane, far more options would have been available.

'The airport lacked the proper ladder for refueling an Airbus as no plane of this make currently lands at Amritsar. This would have been sufficient reason in dallying over refueling and there is no way the plane could have taken off with the bowser connected with the plane.

'Secondly, the very mechanism that allows for the refueling of a plane also allows its "de-fueling" or extraction of fuel from the tank. Also, once the cabinet secretary and the principal secretary contacted officials in the control room, the local authorities immediately assumed a passive role. They were merely passing on information and awaiting instructions. The only active decision taken in Amritsar was to refuel, and that was just before the cabinet secretary called.'

'Captain Sharan's messages about the hijackers being armed with guns and grenades, and the death of four passengers only created panic in the ATC,' says Gill. Punjab Police commandos were three hundred meters from the plane, but the authorities did nothing, fearing that the lives of nearly two hundred persons would be endangered. When they heard four people had died, they still did nothing.

'They were obviously willing to waste four lives through delay and indecision over the refueling but were not willing to take direct action that would risk more lives of the passengers,' says Gill. 'They should have foreseen, or at least taken into account the possibility that Lahore would, at some point of time, grant permission for the plane to land there. To place unqualified faith in Pakistan in such a situation is certainly less than wise.'

After forty-nine minutes on the tarmac, sometimes stationary, sometimes taxiing up and down at low speeds with a gun at his head, Captain Sharan took off, narrowly missing the oil tanker with trained policemen in it, and without permission from the ATC. It was the sorriest moment of the hijacking crisis, and the most unexpected. All of India watched as the A300 revved up, slowly gathered speed and took off. There was nothing anyone could do. By landing at Raja Sansi, Captain Sharan had ensured the authorities had a wonderful opportunity—and now, it was gone. The airfield was empty and all the planning and rushing around had come to naught.

The saddest story is the delay in moving the National Security Guard to Amritsar. The NSG at Manesar, Haryana, was informed at 6.10 p.m., well after it was clear that the A300 was landing at Raja Sansi. The commandos should have been alerted at 5.30 p.m. when cabinet secretary Prabhat Kumar first heard of the hijacking. The commandos took off from Palam Airport at 7.55 p.m., long after they were alerted and just as Captain Sharan was taking off again. What was the point if IC 814 had already left? A brigadier from the 52nd Special Action Group and 130 commandos arrived at Raja Sansi Airport at 8.15 p.m. This was twenty-six minutes after IC 814 had left Amritsar, seventy-four minutes after it landed at Amritsar, and three hours and twenty-five minutes after the ATC at New Delhi received reports of the hijacking. By then, the plane was in Lahore!

The commandos had been ready to take off at 7.05 p.m. on an IAF plane and were only waiting for the negotiators to join them. None did till much later. C.K. Sinha of RAW eventually arrived but a second negotiator couldn't make it. NSG director Nikhil Kumar stated that he cleared the commandos' flight at 7.40 p.m. when the CMG declared they needed the storm troopers more than the negotiators. But a second plane should already have been made available anyway. Of course, a negotiator's presence can be crucial, but did the commandos have to wait for them? The Contingency Plan speaks of negotiators helping the CMG on the hijacking. But if they were that important, why did the CMG eventually ask the commandos to leave without them? After all, there were good people already in place in Amritsar—and they had kept the plane on the ground for forty-nine minutes!

'This is more than amazing—in a situation of extreme emergency, a rapid response team sits waiting for a psychologist to arrive for half an hour and it does not strike the decision makers that the latter could follow on another plane later, if needed,' comments Gill. He calls it 'an abject collapse of basic common sense. In any case, the one-hour lapse between being informed and being ready to take off itself speaks poorly of the efficiency of the NSG. Not factoring the distance to the airport and the traffic on Delhi's roads into a rapid response plan displays an unacceptable level of incompetence.'

The authorities had erred, and the passengers and crew and the people of India would pay for it. No one in New Delhi, Chandigarh or Amritsar ever imagined the plane would leave Raja Sansi Airport. If the A300 did have the extra fuel, perhaps the Delhi winter fog was to blame. In the chaos of Tribhuvan International Airport, Kathmandu, the Captain and flight engineer had taken a fateful decision.

'Make sure there's extra fuel in the aircraft. We may have to circle around a bit in case there is low visibility,' Captain Sharan had told Mr Jaggia. And he had agreed. If Captain Sharan hadn't been as careful, there really may not have been enough fuel to take off. Or even if there were, the plane would have crashed before Lahore.

The CMG couldn't have known about the decision at Kathmandu; all they had were Captain Sharan's frantic messages for refueling. At 6.04 p.m., he had said he had an hour's fuel. At exactly 6.18 p.m., he said, 'We have only forty minutes' fuel.' At 6.32 p.m., he had fuel for flying fifteen minutes and six minutes later, he had enough for twenty-five minutes. The CMG overlooked these contradictory statements. As Gill points out, 'It should have been clear that his words were not reflecting, and were not intended to reflect the true picture regarding the amount of fuel in the plane.'

Instead, the CMG should have been able to deduct that these statements were a strategic device Sharan was using. The plane was being tracked on radar, and its speed was known. The CMG probably did not think that the plane had enough fuel to take off for another airport. They also did not believe that the hijackers, after being turned down once by Lahore, would have another crack at landing there.

Long after the passengers had returned from Kandahar, Brajesh Mishra maintained that by not launching a commando operation, the government avoided carnage. A mere delay in refueling at Amritsar led to the stabbing of two passengers. Thus, the hijackers would have killed more passengers if the commandos had mounted a rescue operation.

But the truth of this speculation will never be known.

Chapter Three

Lahore

24 December 1999

The flight from Amritsar to Lahore—it's just a few minutes really—was the longest flight of my life. I wasn't sure there would be enough fuel. We could have crashed. There was the gun. I still remember the feel of cold metal at the back of my neck, pointed at me, there was that smell of fear in the cockpit. If the ATC at Lahore kept the runway closed, we would be forced to crash-land.

The runway was still closed. This time, we had no option. Both tanks were nearly empty—the reserve lights were blinking. I was yelling at the ground controller at Lahore. I knew he was tracking me on the radar, he had to know what height I was flying.

'We are out of fuel. They're aiming a gun at me. If you don't allow us to land, the plane will crash.'

I didn't get permission. I couldn't find the runway. The lights were off. I had no navigational aids. The city was lit up with hundreds of pink and orange lights for some festivity. I spotted a road and came down and decided on an emergency landing. Then I noticed it was a marketplace. 'Let me not kill these people,' I told myself. I climbed a bit and began circling around. I would have to act very quickly.

'We are virtually out of fuel. We're going to crash now,' I told the hijackers.

'Where are we? Lahore?' Chief asked.

'Yes.'

'Okay, you can crash.'

I knew for sure then that they were not concerned about whether they lived or died, or about any of the innocent passengers on board.

At last, the ATC at Lahore cleared me.

'You can land now,'he told me. 'The runway lights are on.'

I had no idea where the runaway was. I had a few seconds, and perhaps not even that, to decide where it was, and I guessed it would be more on the right. Climbing a little and turning, I saw the approach lights. I knew I wouldn't normally have enough fuel to get there. I turned the plane around sharply so that I would be in landing position within a minute. I was looking out the window, I wanted to locate the runway precisely. Just at the beginning of the runway, there were two red lights and two orange lights. They were 'moving lights', unlike in India, where the lights usually resemble an arrow. Then, I was over the runway, hardly a hundred feet above the tarmac, and both my reserve lights were blinking. There was that jerk of touching down and almost immediately, one of the engines shut down—there was no fuel left. We had made it, but barely.

The 173 hours that we spent in captivity were a difficult period. But there was no moment more hair-raising than the one before landing at Lahore. It was touch-and-go. But even after the successful landing, I couldn't sit back and savor the moment. The hijackers were still pointing their guns at me. There was no sense of fulfilment, only of failure. I had not yet recovered from my intense disappointment that the plane had not been stopped at Amritsar.

Added to that, there was a sense of insecurity and of deep disquiet for me. We were in a hostile country. But I was almost relaxed because it was no longer in my hands. In the darkness, I saw about twenty armed security men advancing towards the plane. They took their positions all around the aircraft, about a hundred feet away.

'How much fuel do we need? Please calculate our requirements,' I told Mr Jaggia.

'We can carry thirty-two tons of aviation fuel,' he replied.

He asked Chief. 'Where do you want us to fly? We need to know that.'

'You fill up the tank. We have to fly for a few hours.' He seemed less stressed now. There was no hint of panic in his voice. At Amritsar, the hijackers were always on the edge, checking the doorways, afraid of a commando operation. Now they were still unsure, but more relaxed.

'Is this Lahore or not?' Chief said. He wanted proof. I had noticed a jeep hovering at the edge of the runway.

I called the ATC. 'Send someone from the jeep near the aircraft. The hijackers will know where we are from what he's wearing.'

A man got off the jeep. He was wearing a black jacket over his white salwar kameez.

Chief wasn't convinced.

'You can get a man to wear anything. I don't believe any of this. I want more evidence.'

I had an idea. The jeep would have Lahore number plates beginning with LA. I pointed this out to the hijackers. They still weren't convinced. The airport authorities sent another vehicle, an open van, again with Lahore number plates. Finally, they seemed convinced.

'Switch off the engines. We want the bowser immediately,' Chief said.

I relayed the message to the ATC.

'It's coming,' he said.

The hijackers were still a little uncertain. Burger was looking out of the cockpit window again and again.

All the Pakistanis wanted to do was pack us off as quickly as possible. Refueling is easy: all you have to do is connect the hose to a panel. They sent a grey and yellow bowser fifteen minutes after landing, but when they attached the bowser to the fuel tank, the pipe began leaking. I immediately informed the ATC, and he promised to send us another bowser. It took a little time, and the hijackers were getting impatient.

'Why isn't the bowser coming?' they asked.

I called up the ATC again.

'Tower. Where is the bowser?' I asked.

'Can you see some lights, two headlights, on your right, about a kilometer away?'

'Yes, I can,' I replied.

I was depressed as I stood behind the flight engineer while Chief checked the panels. I would be asked to take off and I didn't know where I would have to go.

I asked the ATC to remove them. The hijackers were getting a little tense about the security guards around the plane.

I turned to Chief. 'Why don't you let the injured and the women and children go?'

'Give me a little time,' he said.

After talking with the other hijackers, he came back. 'Yes, we'll let the women and children go. Why don't you tell the ATC?'

I called the ATC. 'We want to offload the injured and the women and children. They have agreed to let about thirty people go.'

They weren't interested. 'You wanted fuel and we've given you fuel. Now please leave,' the ATC said.

I asked again. 'Please take our injured passengers.'

'Please leave. Take off immediately.'

I felt terribly disappointed. Even when I had managed to persuade the hijackers, the authorities would not cooperate.

Chief was after me again. 'Why don't you take off from here?'

'We're in the middle of the runway. The plane has to taxi for a while before it can pick enough speed to take off.'

He was still uncertain. 'Don't try to be brave,' he warned.

'Where do you want us to go?'

'You take off first.'

'We can't do that. We must prepare a flight plan and inform the ATC, who will clear us.'

Chief thought for a while. 'Okay. Take us to Kabul.'

I contacted the ATC again. 'They want to go to Kabul. Please tell me the way.'

I was praying for a miracle. Please God, do something so that I don't have to go to Kabul. I was trying to avoid Afghanistan. I tried to muster up arguments for not going there.

'There are no night-landing facilities there. We can't fly to Kabul,' I said.

'*Aapko Kabul hi chalna padega.* (You have to go to Kabul.)'

'Why are you going to Kabul?' Mr Jaggia suddenly asked Chief. 'Let's fly to Geneva. It is a neutral country. Let's fly to London. Or to Italy.'

'Let's fly anywhere else. The people at Kabul may not support you,' Rajinder Kumar said.

Chief listened quietly. 'I know where to go.'

The ATC started telling me about flying to Kabul.

'Change over to Lahore radar,' he said.

We prepared to take off again.

In the past, President Zia-ul-Haq had intervened and stopped hijackers, but under the Pervez Musharraf government, Pakistan was willing only to do nothing. This was after the confrontation in Kargil six months earlier; and even if individual Pakistani officials were ready to help, they were discouraged from doing so. The hijacking was India's problem and for India to solve. Pakistan would not go out of its way to help.

A senior Home Ministry official had a strange story to narrate. The external affairs minister, Jaswant Singh, spoke to his Pakistani counterpart, Abdus Sattar, in Islamabad, twice during the evening. The first time, the latter was very cooperative, and he said he would do whatever was necessary. But he said that he would have to call Lahore from Islamabad in order to arrange things. The next time Singh called, Sattar seemed a different man. He wasn't very cooperative, and it was almost as if he was 'reading out a prepared statement on the phone.' The official said that it was as if he had got orders not to cooperate with the Indian government.

Singh also called the US deputy secretary of state, Strobe Talbott, to speak to Islamabad. It was Christmas Eve in Washington DC, but the state department officials at Foggy Bottom tried their best to help. So did the US ambassador in Islamabad, who requested the Musharraf government to help India through the crisis.

Pakistani officials agreed to the US request. They said they would try to stop the hijackers. The Indian high commissioner to Islamabad, G. Parthasarathy, would be provided with a helicopter to fly to Lahore and speak to the hijackers.

The actual events, however, did not indicate such willingness to help. In Lahore, the authorities did not switch on the runway lights for a long time. Pakistani commandos surrounded the plane, and Pakistani officials refused to accept the passengers that the hijackers were willing to release. Parthasarathy had requested a helicopter just as the hijacked plane landed at Lahore after 8 p.m. His helicopter was ready only at 10.30 p.m. and as he got on, the pilot told him the plane had already left Lahore. A joyride to Lahore wasn't the point; Parthasarathy got off the chopper and returned home. Pakistani officials were speaking in two voices: they would help, and they wouldn't help. A Pakistani foreign ministry official had called the Indian high commission to condemn the incident, but no accurate information was available from Islamabad or Lahore. The Pakistanis wanted to know the identity of the hijackers, but they appeared to back-pedal when they were told about the dead passengers on board. In the end, Pakistan did too little to stop IC 814. And they were too late. The A300, refueled at Lahore, took off for Kabul.

'The Pakistanis,' said Chaman Lal Gupta, minister of state for civil aviation, 'went back on their word. Now that the hijackers have a full tank, they may be heading for a distant place if they are not allowed to land in Kabul.'

In Pakistan, Brigadier Rashid Qureshi, the military spokesman, felt nothing more could have been done. 'We asked them to let the women and children go. But they refused.'

As we headed for Kabul, via Dera Ismail Khan, we contacted the authorities on high-frequency sets. I had taken out the charts—landing in Kabul seemed difficult. I had never been there.

'Kabul. This is 814. We have been hijacked and are heading towards Kabul,' Rajinder said.

The reply from Kabul ATC was very faint: 'Night landing facilities not available. Kabul is closed for you.'

This reply was a relief. I didn't have to fly to Afghanistan and, just as important, handle the Kabul airfield at night.

'What do we do now?' I asked the hijackers.

'Let me speak to Kabul,' demanded Burger. But we could not get a conversation going. There was too much static. The hijackers seemed momentarily undecided about what to do next.

'*Chalo, Kabul nahi jana hain* (Good, we don't have to go to Kabul),' Rajinder said.

'Let's persuade them to go somewhere else. We don't want to go to Afghanistan,' Mr Jaggia said. 'Let's try and ask them to order us to Europe or the Gulf. There's no hope in Afghanistan.'

Chief came back after conferring with the others. 'Do you have enough fuel to go to the Emirates?'

'Yes,' all of us said together. I was relieved. We wanted to fly to the Emirates. And that's where we were going. Rajinder gave me a sly thumbs-up sign.

'*Achcha hua* (That's good),' said Mr Jaggia.

I called Lahore ATC. 'We are not going to Kabul. We want permission for Dubai.'

Shortly after, Lahore ATC got back to me. Kabul was closed, but Kandahar was open. If we wanted, we could have gone to Kandahar that night. This was a conversation that Chief did not hear. As a precautionary measure, I had reduced the volume of the radio set. We wanted to avoid Afghanistan at any cost. If Chief had got wind of such a possibility, there would have been no Al Minhad, no ray of hope, no release of passengers.

There was silence in the cockpit as we turned the aircraft towards Dubai. I put the plane on autopilot; I needed to use the toilet. I also wanted to see what was happening in the cabin. On my way to the toilet at the end of the executive class, I noticed Satnam Singh and Ripin Katyal; they both seemed to be in some discomfort.

'Go inside,' said Bhola, who was standing between the economy class and the executive class. I could not see what was happening in the economy class section.

'Why don't you help this passenger?' I said, looking at Ripin Katyal. 'He needs bandages. Give him some water at least.'

'If you don't go inside, I'll shoot you.'

Chapter Four

Dubai

25 December 1999

We were approaching Dubai, short of fuel as usual. It had been a long flight. I got in touch with the UAE radar. 'Dubai airport is closed for you. You can land at Al Minhad,' the authorities said.

'Where is Minhad? I have never heard of it.'

'It is sixty kilometres south of Dubai. It's an air force base.'

We came down to 2,500 feet. The words 'air force base' had reassured me, and I began to feel optimistic. I thought the authorities had prepared everything. As soon as we touched down, the commandos would storm the plane. Our ordeal would be over. That's why they're moving us to Al Minhad. Dubai and Sharjah are busy airports: a rescue operation would be difficult at either of those places, I thought.

With Chief looking over our shoulders, I couldn't speak to Rajinder and Mr Jaggia. They were also thinking of commando operations, I learnt later.

We were now in touch with Al Minhad ATC. It was nearly 1.30 a.m. when we landed. Relief washed over me. It was a beautiful airfield and probably the commandos weren't too far away.

Chief again panicked as the plane taxied down the runway. 'Stop, stop,' he said.

'I have tried to tell you before,' I said. 'This isn't a vertical-take-off-and-landing jet. The plane must taxi for a while.'

He wouldn't allow me to stop the engines. 'Move the aircraft around,' he said. 'Keep the engines running till we tell you.'

'Al Minhad, this is IC 814. We want to refuel.'

'We have a small bowser here. You'll have to wait. Tell me how much fuel you need. We'll have to ask the main airport.'

I tried to explain to Chief that a small bowser would be of no use, but he did not want to listen. He wanted the plane to be refueled immediately.

So, I contacted the ATC.

'Send whatever you have.' I also told them we had a few injured passengers on board, and women and children. The hijackers were willing to let them go…

'We are sending a van immediately.'

Chief refused. 'We want fuel first. We'll release the women and children only after that.'

'How many people are you planning to let go?' I asked.

'Thirty. We had said thirty at Lahore. But only after we refuel.'

For the Indian government, Al Minhad was another opportunity to stop the hijackers, but absolutely the last one. Delays had prevented a rescue at Amritsar and the authorities hadn't been receptive at Lahore. Now the UAE was the only remaining hope. Otherwise, it seemed inevitable that the aircraft would be taken to Afghanistan and negotiations would be with the Taliban, a diplomatic minefield as India still officially recognized the previous Burhanuddin Rabbani government. There were no Ariana Afghan Airlines flights to India. The Taliban was still a pariah in the international arena; only Pakistan, Saudi Arabia and the UAE recognized the Mullah Omar government. The official Afghan ambassador to New Delhi was a representative of the Rabbani government. Though the Taliban, strongly entrenched with Pakistani help, remained in control of Kabul and most of the country, the Rabbani forces led by Ahmed Shah Massoud held certain areas of northern Afghanistan. In the past, there was talk of a 'Northern Alliance' and the Russians and India had quietly helped Massoud's forces.

At the best of times, landing at Dubai would have been difficult for a hijacked plane—the UAE has a history of refusing permission under such circumstances. Dubai at midnight during Ramadan was impossible, but the Indian ambassador to the UAE, K.C. Singh, tried. He contacted General Sheikh Mohammed bin Rashid al Maktoum, crown prince and defense minister of the UAE.

In New Delhi, the authorities suspected IC 814 would land in Kabul after all. Having been contacted, airport authorities at Kabul said, late in the evening, the plane was due there at 11.30 p.m., two hours after it took off from Lahore.

There was better news later when the authorities called up Kabul again. Yes, the aircraft was turned away. It would land at Dubai. Jaswant Singh spoke to Strobe Talbott again. Could the US state department persuade the UAE to allow a commando operation? For the second time in the evening, the NSG commandos were alerted, though it was a long shot.

It would be a long night, and initially, it was still uncertain where the plane would land.

The news trickled in gradually. Muscat ATC refused permission. Dubai followed suit. The hijacked plane was still homeless.

For the CMG (with L.K. Advani supervising operations from late that evening), Dubai was the best option. India had good relations with them. But they remained unhappy about letting a hijacked plane in till Talbott called the crown prince, as did Singh. In Washington DC, senior officials in Foggy Bottom worked the phones. Assistant Secretary of State Robert Einhorn, officer on special duty (south and south-east Asia) Matt Daley, and Michael Sheehan of the counter-terrorism unit were talking with the UAE officials.

Advani asked if there was a chance of a rescue operation. It was decided to check with the UAE authorities but this time, the NSG would not delay. The commandos, waiting at Amritsar, would fly to Dubai.

'Can I switch off the engine?' I asked Chief.

'Not till the bowser arrives,' he replied.

They were very nervous. They might have been aware that a rescue attempt was possible. At Al Minhad, as in Amritsar, there was a road parallel to the runway, and whenever a car or jeep went past the plane, they ordered me to move the plane.

After about twenty minutes, a new ATC took over.

'I am Abdullah. Let me see what I can do for you,' he said. He sounded cheerful and even better, very, very supportive. It seemed he was on our side. His was the first friendly voice I had heard in a long time. I felt better talking to him. At last, there seemed to be somebody outside trying to help us.

'We will give you fuel only when you give us some passengers,' were his opening words.

Abdullah debated with Chief, who stood over my seat while Burger leaned out of my window looking for commandos. I waited behind the flight engineer's seat.

'You give us the fuel first. Then we'll release some passengers. We trust you...you have to trust us,' Chief said.

But Abdullah wouldn't relent. 'You first release some passengers, then, serve a meal to the ones left behind. Only then will you get fuel.' Then he agreed to send the small bowser, which I knew would not really be of much use as the pipe wouldn't reach the fuel tank. It was more a gesture, I thought.

'Can you see a light? Your bowser is coming,' Abdullah said.

I could see it and immediately turned to Chief. 'You didn't believe him. See, he's sent the bowser.'

It came towards the aircraft and stopped about five hundred feet away.

Chief peered out and objected immediately, 'There should be just two people on the bowser; just the driver and another man.' He was still afraid of a rescue mission.

But Abdullah had his argument ready. 'We need four people to refuel a plane.'

'Well, three is the maximum we will allow,' Chief said. One man got off the bowser. All of them wore khaki uniforms, the bowser was a faded olive green. They were military men, I thought. The bowser approached the plane and stopped just by the cockpit. The hijackers counted the men on the bowser. There were only three. 'Okay, start,' Chief said.

As I had thought, we were wasting our time with a small bowser. The pipe couldn't reach the wing.

'*Ab kya karna hain*? (What do we do?)' asked Chief.

'Didn't I tell you? We must have a bigger bowser,' I replied.

Abdullah was on the line. He said a bigger bowser had been sent from Dubai. 'That's twenty kilometers away. These vehicles move slowly. It will take another forty minutes.'

'Please release the injured passengers,' I requested Chief.

He was unyielding. 'Not till we get fuel.'

Burger was still prowling around, checking for commandos. Chief continued questioning me.

'How much fuel do you have?'

'Very little, about five tons.'

'Okay, take off. *Crash kar do.* How far is the sea?'

I thought of a plan, a plan which I thought would work. After Mr Jaggia pressed the fire-bell on his right, I would steer the plane off the runway into the sand, where I hoped the wheels would get stuck. Once that happened, it would take more than all the king's horses and all the king's men to get the plane back on the tarmac and also flight ready. It would help to buy time, lots of time. As I saw it, it was our last chance, the only chance anti-hijacking squads would have had. And, if nothing else, there would be a better opportunity of negotiating with Burger and gang.

I had to explain things to Chief, answer his very worrying question. 'Quite close.'

'Okay, into the sea she goes.'

'What's the point? The bigger bowser will be here.'

'No, the people here are like the ones in Amritsar.'

I talked to Abdullah again. 'The hijackers are getting impatient. They want me to take off and crash the plane.'

'You have my guarantee—the bigger bowser is coming. You can't lose patience,' he said.

I still hoped for rescue. The delay is deliberate, I thought, as I had at Amritsar. They are readying for action. This was what the hijackers were afraid of. They wanted all lights switched on. I looked around. There wasn't anyone in sight.

Abdullah called again. 'Can you see a light at the end of the runway?'

It was the bowser, slowly coming towards us. I could see it clearly—the shiny yellow paint, the markings in Arabic.

'Our bowser has arrived. You must keep your part of the bargain.'

'Where's the fuel?' Chief answered.

'The fuel is ready. Everything is ready. What if you refuel and fly off? Why don't you make some sort of gesture? Then we'll know you're ready to release the passengers,' Abdullah said.

But Chief was unwilling to compromise. 'If you don't refuel the plane, we will start killing the passengers.'

'Okay. But you must promise to release some passengers,' Abdullah reminded him.

'I promise,' Chief finally relented. 'We'll release the ladies and children. But first, refuel the plane.'

The bowser was edging closer. Abdullah tried again, 'We need an assurance from you.'

'First, tell us how many people you have in the bowser.' There were four people.

'Why four people?' Chief asked.

'We need four people for this bowser,' Abdullah replied.

All four were military men and apparently incapable of refueling the plane. When Chief asked why trained men hadn't come along, Abdullah had an answer ready.

'You asked for a bowser, you didn't ask for men.'

When Chief demanded that the authorities refuel the plane, Abdullah suggested that the flight engineer help out. I thought these were all delaying tactics, attempts to wear out the hijackers. The commandos, I thought, were preparing to strike.

Shankar, gun in hand, escorted Mr Jaggia out. As the refueling began, I gradually started to lose hope.

Abdullah was back on the line. 'We'll remove the bowser only after you release some passengers.'

They did release passengers, but hurriedly; some women and children, but not all of them, and Satnam Singh as well as the dead body of Ripin Katyal. Burger told me he was still alive. I later learnt he was already dead. From the cockpit, I saw the passengers getting off.

'We've released twenty-seven people,' Chief said. I wasn't allowed to move. This was the first time I had a chance to see the passengers. I could see them streaming out, still tense. Some of them had blankets draped over their clothes like shawls. Well, a few lucky ones are out. At least, a few are safe, I told myself.

Abdullah continued to try to negotiate with Chief. 'Sure, you've released some passengers, but what about some food for the others?'

I thought this was the moment we were waiting for. The commandos would come with the meals. I could see the lights of three catering vans. It was about 3 a.m.

'Can the catering van come closer?' Abdullah asked.

'Only one can come,' said Chief.

One came up right next to the plane. 'How many people have you sent?'

'Three,' said Abdullah.

'We want only two,' Chief said.

Burger and Doctor burst into the cockpit.

'We don't want food. The vans probably have security men in them.'

Chief was undecided. He thought about it and then came to a decision. He wanted the trays placed on the tarmac.

I told Abdullah.

He pretended to be livid. 'This is a breach of promise. How can you do that?'

'Everyone is hungry,' the flight engineer said. 'You are, we are, the passengers are.'

The hijackers thought they sensed danger. 'No, no, we don't want the food on board,' Burger said. He seemed to be the most intelligent of the lot and often advised Chief. He went back to the cabin.

'Start the engines. Move, move,' Chief said.

Burger returned. Each time he came in, he seemed more fanatical than ever. He had found five life jackets, he told Chief.

'Why on earth do you need life jackets?' I asked him.

'That's none of your business,' he said. 'Can you swim?'

'Yes.'

Rajinder and Mr Jaggia said they couldn't. I thought they must be planning something terrible, like blowing up the plane as it flew over the Arabian Sea.

I could see a lot of vehicles on the runway. Two of the catering vans had moved a little closer. I could also see an ambulance and a bus that had come to pick up the released passengers. The runway was blocked.

'Start the engines,' Chief said.

I begged him, 'Please, let's wait a while. The passengers need a meal and besides, the runway is blocked.'

I was still hoping against hope. Maybe, if they could stay another hour at Al Minhad, our nightmare would be over. Someone would do something.

'Move. Start the engine,' Chief demanded.

Rajinder punched the yellow start button on the overhead panel, one of the engines rumbled back to life. I pulled the fuel lever and started the second engine.

Abdullah sounded alarmed. 'What are you doing?'

'I have orders to move. I have been told not to stay here for another minute.'

'How can that be?' he told Chief, sounding indignant. 'The passengers have to eat!'

Chief asked me to take off. 'Move, move,' he said. That was one of the two English words he knew; the other was 'stop'. I opened power and the plane began taxiing. The catering vans and the stepladder were still on the tarmac.

On the right was a taxi-track. 'Can I go straight for a bit and then turn?' I asked them. It wasn't easy maneuvering such a big plane.

The flight engineer and I had the fire-alarm ace up our sleeve. I had spoken with him, and we had planned to make the fire alarm go off in case the hijackers forced us to move. It usually goes off automatically, but there was a switch on the flight engineer's panel. Thus, we would abort their plan of making us leave the UAE.

When the hijackers were not in the cabin, I had even told Abdullah I would 'reject' a take-off.

It nearly worked, but for Burger. It was almost as if knew what we wanted to do. As I opened power, he entered the cockpit and stood between the flight engineer's seat and his overhead panel.

Mr Jaggia tried one more time. 'Don't stand here during take-off. It is dangerous. You may fall and hurt yourself.'

I tried as well. 'Mr Burger, please sit in the cabin.' But we couldn't persuade him to move. With that, our forlorn hope crumbled. Now we would have to fly to Kabul. I thought how ironical it was that I should be in Dubai and under such circumstances on Christmas Day, when I had planned to be in nearby Sharjah, celebrating with my family. I thought of a last desperate argument to persuade Chief. The wings were unfortunately higher than the vehicles around, about thirty feet from the ground. They went over the buses. But I thought it was worth a try.

'Chief sahab, these vehicles are on the runway. We might crash into them...' I pointed out.

'It doesn't matter. A small accident won't make a difference. We must fly out of here.'

The runway length available was only 5,000 feet. We were almost in the middle of the runway. I told them it wouldn't be easy to take off from here.

'If you can't take off, crash on the runway,' he replied.

I was desolate; this was the third time that I had hoped for rescue. Amritsar, Lahore and now, Al Minhad. No one could stop us now. There was no hope left. We would have to fly to Kabul. And no one would help us there.

I had to turn the aircraft around. I needed the full length of the runway to take off. I asked Chief for permission.

This time he agreed. 'Yes, but don't do anything rash. Or we'll blow up the plane. Please remember we have to return the plane to the Indian government after we go around the world. It will be our millennium gift to India. Captain sahab, don't worry about it.'

It seemed very strange they spoke so respectfully 'Captain sahab, Flight engineer sahab' but there was always a gun pointing at us!

At times, even now, the memory of the gun on my neck comes back. It was an odd feeling, something cold and sharp and painful. But the way they kept saying 'millennium gift' made me feel suspicious. Were they planning to blow up the plane?

I started to turn the plane. I got a feeling that Abdullah was trying to delay my take-off by not ordering the vehicles off the runway. I tried to take some more time, backtracking and going through an extra flight control check. We were at one end of the runway.

'You will not stop,' Chief said.

Abdullah tried one last time. 'What are you doing? You're not keeping your promise!' He sounded alarmed, almost desperate.

'They are going to shoot me if I don't take off. I can't do anything. I am taking off.'

Again, we went past the catering vans and buses, and as we reached 160 knots, we took off. It took some skill, and a bit of luck helped. But we were off again.

Mr Jaggia and I had succeeded in playing one trick though. We had deliberately altered the settings of the fuel tank in such a way that the plane could not be refueled any more. The next stop would be our last. All the aviation fuel would gush out and we would say the mechanism was damaged. This was the only measure we had managed to pull off, and it was meagre comfort indeed.

It was nine hours after the hijacking when the IC 814 touched down at Al Minhad. Among the people present at the airport was the crown prince of Dubai. It was just after 1.30 a.m. IST. If there had to be a rescue operation by Indian commandos, with some help from the security forces of Dubai, just before dawn, it would require pressure from the US on the desert kingdom. Strobe Talbott spoke to the ruling family. The crown prince had virtually ruled out the possibility of Indian commandos intervening if there were an operation; the UAE federal forces would do the needful, he told the Indian government. Present at Al Minhad along with the crown prince was Lieutenant-General Sheikh Mohamed bin Zayed Al Nahyan, the UAE armed forces chief. Indian Embassy officials weren't allowed inside the base. But there was hope that some action might be taken: foreign secretary Lalit Mansingh, after his discussions with the US ambassador in New Delhi, Richard Celeste, told the government that the Americans were doing their best and, if possible, would ensure that the plane did not take off.

After discussions with the US consul general in Dubai, a passengers-and-food-for-fuel swap was decided on. There would be no commando operation, but they would ask for the release of the seventy women and children on board and the others would be provided with food and water. In the end, only twenty-six passengers, including the injured Satnam Singh, were released and the dead body of Ripin Katyal was flung down a chute.

At Al Minhad, Geeta Baisala remembers a few women with children were asked to get up and sit in the executive class. 'I thought they would make us sit somewhere else. There, they asked us to pick up our handbags and leave.'

'Where is your baby?' a hijacker asked her as she was getting off. She told him Kirti was covered by her shawl. He asked her to hurry up.

'We thought everyone was being let off. We were waiting when they threw out some luggage. And then a body was flung out of the plane. That's when we realized we were the only people to be released. There were a lot of tears, a lot of women had left their husbands, and in some cases, their children, on the plane. I didn't know where I was. I knew we were in a Middle Eastern country. I saw men in white robes. Then a man came up and introduced himself. He was from the Indian Embassy. I was really relieved. I burst into tears. "We will be with Papa very soon," I told my children.'

When the hijackers announced that women with children could get up, Indu Verma stood up, her daughter in her arms, and went to where her husband was sitting with her son. She took her son by the hand, glanced sideways at her husband, still looking down as ordered by the hijackers, and walked out of the plane.

'I only came to know about Ripin Katyal after I got to Dubai,' she said.

There were others who were blissfully unaware of the hijacking all the way to Dubai. Till she was freed, Kasturi Meena had no idea that the plane had been hijacked. The delays, the hijackers told her, were because of engine trouble. And she thought Burger and the others were petty dacoits who were after the passengers' jewelry. Surprised to see Arabs in white robes, she asked in Hindi where they had landed. It was then that embassy officials explained what had happened.

Civil Aviation Minister Sharad Yadav flew to Dubai in a special plane on Christmas Day. He received the first batch of released hostages and escorted them to India, and conveyed the Vajpayee government's thanks to the UAE. A passport had to be hurriedly readied for him before he left as this was his first trip abroad. It was initially planned that the relatives of the released passengers would accompany him. But this idea was later dropped.

After Yadav landed at Dubai, he met the passengers who told him of the first hours on the plane, about the weapons on board, the threats and the violence. A compensation of 5 lakh rupees for the Katyal family was in order, the minister felt. But the Indian Embassy officials disagreed, and no announcement was made. After thanking the UAE government, he returned with the passengers and the wooden casket carrying the body of Ripin Katyal late in the evening.

Chapter Five

Kandahar

25 December 1999

'Change over to Dubai radar,' the Al Minhad ATC said. 'What are your intentions?' Dubai ATC asked.

Chief prompted me.

'Kabul. Please give me instructions,' I said.

We changed to the UAE radar and then Muscat control. We were flying comfortably at 29,000 feet, but I had never been so miserable. I'd rather the plane crashed than fly to Kabul, I told myself.

Burger, who had gone into the cabin, came back into the cockpit again. 'How far is the sea from here?' he asked.

'Why?'

'I want to know.'

'We don't fly over the sea,' I answered, lying badly.

'We flew over the sea when we came,' he argued.

'Yes, we did. We must take a different route when we are flying back.'

Rajinder took out a Jeppesen air-route map. 'Look at this map. Where's the sea?' he asked. He was hoping Burger couldn't read maps.

Mr Jaggia also joined in, 'No, no. We don't fly over the sea.'

For all our misery about going to Kabul, we didn't want Burger to order us to crash into the sea or to blow the plane up. Over these hours we had come to recognize that he was the hothead, the extreme fanatic.

Burger was insistent. 'We flew over the sea the last time. Why can't we take the same route?'

'We have to take a different route,' I explained. We were taking the same route. Thank God, it was still dark!

He finally believed me. 'Okay. *Koi baat nahin*.'

Dawn was breaking as we headed north, crossing Alpore. We were still flying over the sea, but they didn't look down, so we were safe.

Then Burger asked another crazy question.

'*Cockpit se neeche jaane ka rasta kahan hain*? (Where is the way down from the cockpit?) How do you get off the plane? Isn't there an emergency opening under the pilot's seat?'

I thought maybe this was how they planned to end it. They would ask us to fly at a lower altitude. Then they would jump off the plane, with or without parachutes, leaving behind a ticking time bomb.

We were now speaking to Karachi ATC and again, Burger interfered. 'You are speaking with Karachi, and you're telling me you're nowhere near the sea? Karachi is a port.'

'Yes, that's true. We have left Karachi behind. We're flying north of Karachi.'

All the hijackers crowded into the cockpit. They seemed relaxed, almost happy, swapping stories.

'How many children do you have?' Burger asked.

'I have two daughters,' I said.

'My daughter is getting married six days from now, on New Year's Eve,' Mr Jaggia said. It wasn't true at all, but we didn't want them to shoot us. These little personal details, we hoped, would make them think twice.

Burger was very curious about the A300's controls.

'How does this work?' he would ask, or 'What is this button for?'

'Can you train him to fly?' Chief asked me, smiling.

'Oh yes, in a couple of days. He's almost a pilot already.'

We flew towards Lahore ATC. I picked up IC 594, a flight from Sharjah to Calicut. Captain S.P.S. Suri was flying, I recognized his voice, talking with Muscat ATC. 'IC 540,' he said, not IC 814. 'What is your endurance and TNB or total number of persons on board?' The code he was using was quite clear to me. He wanted to know how much longer I could fly and how many people I had on board. I knew it was a message for me; IC 540 is the evening flight to Chennai from New Delhi! He obviously wanted to know how I was. I was wearing headphones. I reduced the volume of the speakers in the cockpit. No one could hear anything. The hijackers were also relaxed. I didn't have to take permission anymore. 'We have 162 on board.' I started weeping. I put my head down and wiped away the tears. I didn't want anyone to see me crying, not my crew, not the hijackers. Here I was, flying to a hostile country, something I had been trying desperately to avoid all night. My plane had landed at Amritsar, Lahore and Dubai, and no one had done anything to save us. I was in deep trouble.

'You haven't brought my uniform,' he said. I was supposed to bring his clothes from Kathmandu to New Delhi.

I couldn't reply. I switched off the radio-transmission set.

I spoke to Lahore control. 'We're heading for Kabul.'

We were flying at 0.78 Mach, over Dera Ismail Khan. They asked me to contact Kabul and I did, on High Frequency, not the usual Very High Frequency.

'Kandahar is open for you, but not Kabul,' they said.

'What do I do? Kabul is closed,' I told Chief.

He went off to consult the other hijackers. He seemed a little crestfallen when he returned. 'Why Kandahar? Why not Kabul?'

'I don't know. I haven't got clearance.'

'Okay, take us to Kandahar.'

Burger, still carrying his revolver and hand grenade, said, 'We have problems in Kandahar. We'd prefer Kabul.'

'I have no choice,' I said, and they agreed.

I contacted Kandahar and told them our estimated time of arrival: 8.15 a.m. IST.

'Welcome to Kandahar,' they said. But I was worried, I didn't know anything about the layout of Kandahar airport—I wouldn't know how to land there. Not being familiar with the layout of an airport can cause problems; if the visibility was poor, I wouldn't be able to land.

At that time, a PIA aircraft was flying over us. I think he had taken off from Kandahar.

'What is the elevation of the airport?' I asked the pilot. I had to know.

'About 3,000 feet.'

'What is the landing procedure?'

'You have to make a visual approach.' He briefed me about the airport and how to land there. If he hadn't been there, I would have had to ask the ATC. They have different approaches to the airport, meaning you can fly in towards the tarmac from different directions. Often, you had to watch out for hand-held rocket launchers or surface-to-air missiles, given the trouble in the area.

Then I contacted Kandahar for clearance to land.

I came down to 22,000 feet and flew at that level till I was only forty miles away. The ATC asked me to descend to 10,000 feet.

'Whenever you have the runway in sight, let us know and land,' he said.

'Your non-directional beacon (NOB) isn't working. You don't have other navigational aids,' I told him. 'How do I reach Kandahar?'

Reaching an unknown destination, that too without adequate navigational aids, was going to be very difficult. Luckily, my plane was fitted with a global positioning system (GPS) and using that, I managed to reach Kandahar. Yet I couldn't find the runway. The whole area looked like an abandoned airfield and the tarmac didn't look any different from its surroundings. My GPS said the airfield was one mile away, and visibility was much more than that. Yet I still couldn't see the runway! Looking down, I saw a few Afghanistan Air Force planes, an AN-12 Russian-made transport aircraft and a few fighters, and a blue and white Ariana Airlines plane parked on the tarmac. Coming down to 5,000 feet, I finally saw the runway and made a visual approach.

As I was coming down, I could see the taxi-track on the left.

The ATC told me: 'The runway is on the right, the taxi track on your left.' It was all very confusing.

'Stop, stop,' Chief said, as usual as we taxied to a halt. So, this was Kandahar, our destination, the last place on earth we wanted to be in. I wondered how long we would be here and whether we would ever leave the place. I felt completely desolate, even defeated.

The airstrip looked derelict, the tarmac was pot-holed and cracked, and loose stones lay scattered all over. I looked around, and I couldn't see a blade of grass. Kandahar was shades of brown—brown hills all around and brown broken ground. It was reminiscent of Leh airfield where I often flew. But Leh had beautiful mountains all around. On my left, I noticed a Toyota open jeep driving towards us; six people in turbans and carrying grenade launchers waved. Chief, sitting right behind me, waved back. He was laughing. The hijackers finally seemed happy and relaxed, they seemed to have come home.

We have hijackers inside and terrorists outside. This is the end. We're finished; we'll never get back, I thought. Chief ordered us out of the cockpit. Burger opened a window and called out to the people in the Toyota. When we came out of the cockpit, the cabin was in shocking state. The galley was a mess. Food trays were lying around, spoons and forks were on the floor. People had been walking all over them. The executive class was empty—there was only the hand luggage of the passengers. Of the seven or eight men who had earlier been brought there, Satnam Singh and Katyal had been left in Dubai, and the rest had been sent back to the economy class.

In the darkened economy class, I saw the passengers for the first time in many long hours. Everyone was blindfolded; they had the seat covers over their heads. They also had their heads down. I went back to the cockpit to speak to Chief.

'You are the chief of the hijackers. I am the chief of the aircraft. I am responsible for the passengers, and I am requesting you to make sure they are comfortable. They shouldn't be blindfolded, and they shouldn't keep their heads down. Also, put the cabin lights on. I will fly where you tell me to within the realms of possibility, but you cannot harm my passengers.'

He agreed.

Pushing my luck, I asked about Rachna Katyal. I still hoped her husband was injured, not dead, though I seriously wondered how someone who had lost so much blood could still be alive. And I wanted her to be released.

'She is only one girl. In Jammu and Kashmir, twenty-five thousand of my sisters have no news of their husbands!' he replied.

It was then that I was told of her husband's death. Chief ordered me, my crew and all the passengers who knew about Ripin Katyal's death to not tell Rachna about it. I thought it was a good idea. I didn't know how long we would have to stay in Kandahar, and I did not want her to face this tragic loss along with the other inevitable hardships. One of the hijackers—I think it was Doctor—hid Ripin's bloodied clothes under a seat in the executive class.

Bhola came forward and asked us to sit down. We sat down amidst the hand luggage in the executive class and whispered to one another.

'We've come to Kandahar. This was their ultimate destination,' I told Mr Jaggia.

'You never know. They may ask us to fly somewhere else,' he replied.

A few minutes later, Bhola ordered us back to the cockpit.

'Speak to the ATC,' Chief said.

'A Pajero is going towards the plane. Just follow it,' the ATC said.

I looked at the hijackers. They were acting as if they had just got home after work and taken their shoes off to relax.

I followed the Pajero across the airfield. It was like driving down a bumpy country road. The tarmac looked as if it hadn't been repaired in a hundred years; or at least since the Russians left in 1987. I could see a lot of aircrafts on my right, many of them smashed up. Many were damaged fighters, probably little more than junk by now. People were lounging around the airfield, or casually walking about. I noticed a lot of people in Taliban regalia: turbaned, carrying grenade launchers. I had never seen such a badly maintained airport. We taxied up to the terminal; Kandahar International Airport, said the sign. Despite the mirrored facade, the terminal looked shabby, even unused.

'You can stop the aircraft,' the ATC said. We were right in front of the terminal and the ATC tower.

I spotted two Ariana Airlines aircrafts, including a very old Russian built AN-12 aircraft. An equally aged fire tender approached, dirty and creaking.

How can such a fire tender ever work, I wondered.

After this, I went back to sit with the rest of the crew. In mid-afternoon, Chief summoned Mr Jaggia. He wanted the plane refueled, he had to fly for five more hours, he said. The flight engineer stonewalled. The refueling system was damaged, he replied.

As I sat in the cabin, in the soft light of early evening, I could see the anxiety on the faces of the passengers. They had questions to ask; they wanted to know where they were and how long the nightmare would last. I didn't have many answers, but I wanted to speak to them, to reassure them as best as I could.

'I want to speak to the passengers on the public address system,' I told Burger. 'Please ask Chief for permission.'

He took me to Chief, who was sitting inside the cockpit. 'I want to speak to the passengers.'

He agreed.

I stood between the executive and the economy classes. 'Ladies and gentlemen. I am Captain Devi Sharan. You must be wanting to know where we are and what will happen now. The chief hijacker has permitted me to speak to you,' I began.

I told them what most knew already that we first went to Amritsar and then took off for Lahore. That the Pakistanis initially refused to allow us to land, but eventually did.

'The hijackers wanted to fly to Kabul, but we were forced to go to Dubai where they released a few passengers. We refueled and reached Kandahar early this morning. Kabul is still closed for us. Right now, we're waiting for a rescue team or people from India. As you know, the hijackers are armed. Please cooperate with them. I don't want anyone to confront them. It is not in our interest. This is my request. Have patience, and I am sure something will happen. I believe in God, and I believe everyone will be safe. So, please don't panic.'

I told them to contact me or my crew in case they had any problems; under the circumstances, it was the best I could do.

One day, Saibal Kar realized, you were human, an entity, part of civilization; the next, as a passenger in a hijacked plane, you were nothing, alive only because the hijackers hadn't cut your throat, you were worse than a slave. To go to the bathroom in the morning, Kar needed permission. When he asked, after lifting his head, Shankar, surly as ever, snarled: '*Hindi me bolo*. (Speak in Hindi.)'

'*Mereko bathroom jana hain* (I need to go to the bathroom),' Kar said.

'*Jao aur phir jaldi wapis aao* (Go, and come back soon),' Shankar replied. Returning, as he sat down, he realized that out there somewhere, away from the snake-pit that was the aircraft's cabin, there was another world, there was hope. He recalls, 'There was a Bengali gentleman on my left; he was getting up, reaching out to push up the window shutter even as Shankar shouted at him. It was all very weird. Shankar, knife in hand, soon realized the man wasn't doing much harm. All he was interested in, as dawn broke over Kandahar, was doing a surya namaskar.'

'Like Burger, Shankar was professionally trained, like a commando you'd say, unlike Bhola, younger, ill-tempered, always on the edge and even, cruel. Once, when Bhola hit a passenger, Burger was there in a flash. He told Bhola to calm down and didn't let him near that part of the plane for a while.'

The hijackers were significantly more relaxed as the day wore on. But we were not, and we were very hungry. Lunch was particularly modest: a bit of rajma and Kandahari naan and it was served very late. The food was placed on the ladder by the ground staff at Kandahar. The hijackers had opened the door on the left-hand side to pick up the food. Burger, who was easily the most sociable of the hijackers in his more pleasant moods, was chatting with the passengers. He came over to us at one point. 'There will be a spread tonight: Kabuli pulao,' he said.

Dinner arrived at 8.30 p.m. and orders rang out in the cabin. 'Everyone put your head down. No one look up.' They opened a door and the chill air of Kandahar swept in. Burger and Shankar carried the food inside. They called Anil Sharma and Satish, the two flight pursers, and asked them to serve. The air hostesses also joined in.

When I had heard of Kabuli pulao, I had visions of a gourmet meal; it was the first meal we were having in a while. But the food itself was disappointing. It was just brown fried rice with a few raisins sprinkled on top, and it was cold.

A little later, Burger emerged again from the cockpit. He wanted batteries, pencil cells, and everyone reached for their cameras and Walkmans. I turned cold with fear. Maybe they were readying a remote-controlled device. They could blow up the plane in the night when we were asleep, I thought. I hoped no one would give them any, but I couldn't stop the passengers. I noticed everyone trying to help them, to ingratiate themselves even. It was as if the passengers felt that they would be spared if they cooperated. If they were on the right side of the hijackers, they thought, they wouldn't be shot. I realized later that it was the beginning of what is called the Stockholm syndrome, where prisoners begin to sympathize with their kidnappers or captors.

Late that night, I was summoned by Chief.

'Did you want us all killed?' he asked. He had been listening to the Voice of America and had heard that K.P.S. Gill had praised me for landing in Amritsar and taken apart the present government and the police for failing to take advantage of this.

'He's only saying this to beat his own drum,' I said, trying to convince Chief.

Then Mr Jaggia was summoned.

'Do you have a satellite phone?' Chief asked. 'If you have one, I want it. Otherwise...'

'No, I really don't have one,' he replied.

'Where is Jaswant Singh getting all this information?'

'About what we said and what we did?'

Mr Jaggia thought for a moment. 'A lot of passengers were released at Dubai. They must have told him,' he said.

This seemed to satisfy Chief, and we were sent back to our seats. We were now sitting towards the front of the economy class section, in the second row.

Sometime later, I was almost dropping off when Burger came back. 'Chief says you need to rest. Come to the executive class.'

I lay down on the executive class seats, Mr Jaggia behind me and Chief just in front. When I woke up four hours later, Chief was asleep.

Could we overpower them while they were resting, I wondered. Then I saw Bhola and Doctor walking around in the dark. Disappointed, I fell asleep again.

With the A300 in Kandahar, the cabinet committee for security met. Prime Minister Vajpayee declared that his government would not bend before such show of terror. President K.R. Narayanan spoke of 'an act of terrorism by desperate men with no respect for human lives.'

The statement from Rashtrapati Bhavan added, 'This again highlights the need for concerted international action to prevent terrorists from holding the world to ransom in the name of whatever cause they claim to espouse. The heinous terrorist action causing death, injury and grievous trauma to innocent passengers needs to be condemned in the strongest terms.'

Yet the Taliban foreign minister, Wakil Ahmed Muttawakil, appeared to be washing his hands of the hijacking. It wasn't his problem, it seemed. 'The Taliban has passed on the demands [of the hijackers] to the United Nations with a request to the world body to negotiate,' was all he would say. Initially, the Taliban spokesman in the UN allowed India till the morning of 27 December to send negotiators.

The diplomatic problems were only beginning. India didn't recognize the Taliban. The Afghan ambassador to New Delhi, Masoud Khalili, belonged to the deposed Rabbani government and he was only too happy to condemn what he called 'barbaric action.' He, of course, suggested that the Taliban were helping the hijackers.

Jaswant Singh continued to blame Nepal for the 'major security lapse at Tribhuvan Airport' and Indian Airlines flights to Kathmandu were suspended indefinitely. 'We are deeply disappointed over serious security lapses that resulted in the hijacking,' he said. There was talk about the cursory passenger security checks and the petty bribes necessary to get contraband into the luggage hold, and about the warning by western intelligence agencies about a possible hijack by Osama bin Laden.

And Kathmandu was half-admitting it. 'Security at the airport was not up to the mark but there was no major lapse by the government,' stated the prime minister, K.P. Bhattarai. The Nepalese government arrested four airport workers for 'aiding' hijackers and suspended all security and customs staff.

In the first hours after the hijacking, no one knew who the hijackers were. The Islamic Salvation Front, a faded outfit if there was one, took responsibility, but that was quickly discounted. The Lashkar-e-Taiba denied any role in the hijacking, and that left the Harkat ul-Ansar, an organization often helped by the Taliban. The Harkat, one of the prominent militant outfits in the Valley, is also supported from across the border. The Al Faran, which is linked to the Harkat, was responsible for the kidnapping of the four Western tourists, who remain untraced, in 1995. As it has strong Pakistani links, Harkat involvement in the hijacking was initially suspected, but that was strengthened after the hijackers wanted Maulana Masood Azhar released. He was a prominent Harkat ul-Ansar ideologue and orator who was arrested in Anantnag, in 1994, and was now in a Jammu jail. Now the authorities were going through the Maulana's file with a toothcomb.

The passengers' families had waited at New Delhi airport and complained bitterly about not being kept informed. They were also growing restive at the government's tardiness in resolving the crisis and arranging for freeing the passengers.

Till she was released along with the other passengers on New Year's Eve, Rachna Katyal didn't know her husband was dead, though she certainly suspected the worst. On Christmas Eve, her family had waited at the Indira Gandhi International Airport lounge all night. The next morning, they heard Ripin Katyal was stabbed to death, because he had dared to look up when the passengers had been asked to keep their heads lowered. Only twenty-five, Katyal had studied engineering and ran an electrical goods agency. His wedding photographs show him to be a studious-looking young man.

His pretty wife is beside him in the photographs, smiling. He had married Rachna on 3 December; the Kathmandu trip was their honeymoon. They had planned to return on 22 December, but they had decided to stay on another two days.

At their Gurgaon residence on Christmas Day, the lights had all gone out. There were children at the gate, playing with make-believe machine guns. Ripin's father heard about his son at the airport and collapsed.

'He would not harm anyone. He was always calm and patient, not the kind of person who is provoked easily or would react violently. It is surprising that they picked on him,' Tarun Katyal, Ripin's cousin, said.

And the torture of waiting wasn't even over for the family. Rachna was still on the plane. They didn't know that she was not aware of her husband's death. The Katyals and Rachna's parents, the Sehgals, asked the government to ask the hijackers to release her. 'We have conveyed a mercy appeal to the government to ask the hijackers to free my sister,' said Sumit Sehgal before the TV cameras at the airport. Ripin's uncle, Mohan Katyal, said, 'We will have to cremate Ripin Katyal in the absence of his wife. We have requested the government to facilitate Rachna's release. We even said we would wait for three days.'

'Our world has been shattered,' said P.K. Vij, another uncle, after hearing about Ripin's death. 'Why can't they let Rachna go?'

The hijackers would refuse till the end.

These were the first signs of unrest from the passengers' families. The government would soon have to face a tidal wave of unhappiness.

Chapter Six

Kandahar

26 December 1999

The early part of that morning was about hope. 'Maybe negotiators are flying in from India. We'll probably be released tonight,' I told Mr Jaggia.

'Would you like some tea?' Rajni, one of the air hostesses, asked. Some things hadn't changed. 'We also made tea for the hijackers.'

'What are you planning?' she whispered as she served us. 'Should we overpower them?'

'Have you seen the weapons they have?' I spoke. 'They'll kill us all if we tried. That's a last option. Let's talk with them and wait for a solution. Maybe something will happen.'

The hijackers summoned Mr Jaggia. They wanted all lights switched off, and they wanted one of their bags retrieved from the hold.

Later that morning, a passenger came to see me. He was tall, about fifty, dressed in a checked shirt and a black jacket. He introduced himself as Roberto. 'I am also a pilot,' he said. This is a man who can help me in an emergency, I thought. He did not talk long but went away and sat right at the end of the cabin.

The passengers were under great stress and very anxious. They were hoping desperately for an early end to the crisis. Some of them clutched the tails of my jacket as I walked down the aisle.

'Sir, did anything happen last night?' one man asked.

'Is the government trying to rescue us?' asked another.

'No, there's nothing. There's no news,' I told them.

Shankar, who was patrolling that part of the cabin, didn't like these interchanges at all. 'When you walk up and down, look straight, not sideways,' he commanded.

In the toilet, I surveyed myself in the mirror. I looked terrible: unshaven, tired and haggard. My troubles are far from over, I told myself, and back in New Delhi, my wife and children were spending sleepless nights. How was Navneet explaining my absence to our daughters, who were too young to understand, I wondered.

I noticed Roberto as I walked out of the toilet. It seemed like he wanted to say something to me. Maybe he knew something about the hijackers that I didn't. I went over to speak with him.

'Which airline?' I asked.

'Swissair.'

Shankar intervened. 'Go to your seat,' he told me. The hijackers had learnt to target me after Lahore. Initially, they thought Mr Jaggia (he is older and looks very dignified and even distinguished) was the captain, but after they hit him at Amritsar, I made it very clear that I am the commander of the plane.

The hijackers had their beats. Chief often sat in the cockpit. Burger roamed around; he would sometimes go in and out of the cockpit. Doctor was mostly at the back during most of our days at Kandahar. Bhola was usually at the back too, and Shankar would stay in front to help Chief and Burger, if necessary.

Usually, the passengers would just be sitting quietly, waiting for things to happen. Words cannot describe how slowly each minute seemed to pass, when we had little to do but brood over our possible fate and try to imagine what was happening to our families, in Delhi and in the world at large. I could only think obsessively of possible rescue efforts.

'Do you think the negotiating team has left?' Rajinder asked me.

'Probably. If they left at 9 a.m., they should be here at 10.30 a.m.' All we could do was sit and hope, there was nothing concrete to do.

Chief called Mr Jaggia. 'Please prepare for departure,' he said.

'I have to know the destination.'

'It's a five-hour flight. Let's go back to Amritsar. We want to destroy the plane on Indian soil.'

'Why?'

'So far, the Indian government hasn't even raised an eyebrow about you.'

Such whimsical changes in plan were very disconcerting for us. We were hoping for a resolution. I knew a UN team had arrived at Kandahar that morning. Burger had informed me of this during his 'flying lessons'. He was as talkative as he was aggressive and would provide me with such little snippets of information.

I always felt that Burger was testing me during these lessons. He would ask questions to check if I was telling the truth. I felt that right after taking off from Dubai and, at times, before take-off. He knew a certain amount about the aircraft, where the fuel gauges and the central instrument panel were, that there was another fuel gauge on the flight engineer's panel. He had asked Mr Jaggia about a cockpit trap door. And then he asked me if I had trained on a simulator. He hadn't learnt to fly, but he clearly had done a cockpit familiarization course. But these lessons were useful for me too, for the information he supplied.

Some time later, I asked to speak to Chief.

Chief was speaking to a UN official about the food to be served to the passengers and crew when I entered the cockpit.

'What do you want to say?'

'I want to appeal to the UN.'

'Okay.'

'I am Captain D. Sharan, commander of Flight 814. This is my appeal and please tell the BBC and CNN about it,' I told the official on the wireless. 'And Star News.'

'Go ahead.'

'Please ask them to appeal to the prime minister of India, Mr Atal Behari Vajpayee, the secretary-general of the UN, Mr Kofi Annan, and everyone else who believes in humanity that they should help us, rescue us. The conditions inside the plane are deteriorating. Please find a solution,' I said. I thanked Chief and returned to my seat.

We were back to our routine of waiting after that.

Chief summoned Mr Jaggia a little later. 'Is the plane ready to fly?' he asked.

'I am not sure. We have had a difficult landing. A lot of fine-tuning is necessary. Besides, there is a refueling problem. We cannot fill the fuel tanks,' he said.

The hijackers didn't know what we had done at Al Minhad. As we had planned, when Mr Jaggia had gone down to help with the refueling, he had reset the panel in such a way that the plane couldn't be refueled again.

'Breakfast is coming. No one look up,' the hijackers announced at about 11 a.m.

Breakfast was two crates of fruit—apples and oranges, not very clean. Burger was in his element. He summoned Sabita and Kalpana, two of the air hostesses. 'Cover your head with your sari pallus before serving the food,' he ordered. That was the standing instruction to them as well as to all the other women. Whenever the door was opened, whenever the Taliban officials were around, they had to cover their heads. Everyone was given an apple, still unripe and a little dusty, and an orange.

I bit into my apple and turned to Mr Jaggia. 'It's nothing to look at, but I've never eaten an apple that is so sweet.'

'Just eat what you get,' he replied. 'Who knows when we're going to eat next?'

'How was breakfast?' asked Burger, a little less threatening this morning.

'*Achcha laga, achcha laga* (It was good, it was good),' all the passengers said. I noticed the passengers would never say anything that would offend the hijackers.

'Have you ever had such wonderful fruit? If you hadn't been on this flight, you would never have tasted such fruit!' he said. I wondered if he was serious.

'Chief has asked for you,' Bhola said, some time later.

He was waiting quietly when I went to the cockpit. 'The UN people want to speak to you about the message you left with them,' he said.

I called the ATC and asked to talk to the UN representative. A man came on the line.

'Yes, Captain. This is the UN representative.'

'Is there a message for me?'

'CNN and the BBC have already broadcast your message.' He added that a team from Islamabad was flying in. The Indian ambassador to Islamabad would also be coming.

'That's a very positive development,' I told Chief. 'This thing will be over this evening!' I asked him whether I could share this information with the passengers, and he agreed to let me do so.

It was just before noon when I stood in front of the passengers, next to the public address microphone. As I got up to speak, everyone was silent, expectant, hoping for the best and probably expecting the worst. I told them I had requested the BBC and CNN to broadcast my message asking for help and that this had been done. I also informed them that the Indian ambassador to Islamabad and several officials would be in Kandahar in a few hours. All was not lost. There was a chance of getting back. Perhaps, we would be free quite soon!

Everyone was thrilled.

Late in the afternoon, the hijackers took pity on us. '*Kabuli pulao aa raha hain* (Kabuli pulao is arriving),' Burger shouted. Lunch would arrive, after all. It didn't make me very happy.

'We had that rubbish last night,' I muttered under my breath. This time, Burger was close enough to hear me.

'This is all that is available here,' he explained.

For Burger, the meals were a bit of a joke. He made fun of the passengers. 'What would you like to eat, ladies and gentlemen? What can I serve you?' he would say.

As if we had any choice. 'No, no, we'll eat whatever is available,' the passengers would say. Burger would insist that 'special khana' was arriving. What he seemed to be consciously doing was to keep the passengers relaxed. If he can joke with us, he's not going to kill us, was the logic that seemed to comfort many of the passengers. In fact, some of the newly married women would be very coy.

'Burger bhaiya, what's for dinner tonight?' they would ask. 'Oh, special khana for you,' he would reply.

The food arrived at about 3 p.m. We kept our heads down as the doors opened. This was standard practice: nobody was to walk to the toilet or even stand up till the doors were shut. Burger and Shankar gave quick orders to two of the air hostesses. They took them to the galley. The two flights pursers followed. This time the meal was in polythene packs: no Kabuli pulao but naans, big cold Kandahari naans, a bit of duck or chicken, and two oranges. There were only a hundred packs; there were 162 of us.

The hijackers took care to ensure that everyone ate. We tore apart the polythene packs and kept aside the oranges for the vegetarians to eat with the naans.

A little later, one of the passengers in the front rows caught hold of me. '*Ab bataiye, ho kya raha hain.* (Now tell me, what's happening.)'

'I've already told you.'

Another man stood up. '*Aapko kya lagta hain*? (What do you think?)' he asked.

'The ambassador will be here. There will be pressure on the government, and everything will be settled by this evening.

Others were beckoning me over. 'Will you come this side, please. I can't hear you,' several people said. I had to tell them the same thing.

Then another passenger, Mr Saibal Kar, stood up. He was one of the more active passengers, who was always doing things. I had to repeat the same thing to him. All through these conversations, Bhola sat quietly. None of the hijackers stopped me at all.

While talking to the passengers, I was on the look-out for people who I thought I could rely on in an emergency or in case we hatched some plans for escape. I noticed someone in one of the middle rows, tall and well-built, sitting with his wife. He was handsome and looked North Indian. I stopped to talk to him.

'*Tussi Punjab de ho*? (Are you from Punjab?)' I asked. '*Takre rehna* (Be brave),' I told him. 'Don't worry too much.' I felt I was taking a risk. What if he was one of the allies of the hijackers who had not yet revealed his affiliations?

I put a hand on his shoulder so that it seemed like a casual conversation, as if I was asking which village or district of Punjab he was from. 'You have to be brave...we have to be brave,' I said in Punjabi. I told him that we needed to be ready for any eventuality. Who knew what would happen? We might need to fight the hijackers.

I had decided to prepare some of the passengers for a possible showdown, but I wouldn't spell things out, only indicate what the possibilities were. I started briefing likely looking passengers. 'Be brave; be prepared for any eventuality,' I told them. I also taught them about handling emergency exits and chutes. I was somewhat apprehensive about doing this. Maybe there were a few more hijackers on the plane, their backup team, quietly waiting to see what we would do.

This was the day when people began to fall ill. Anil Khurana, one of the passengers, had high blood sugar. There were three doctors on board and miraculously even insulin injections were available—one of the other patients was carrying some. Samant Brara also fell ill. He had a terrible stomach ache. Both men were taken to the now empty executive class and made to lie down.

Khurana's condition deteriorated so much that eventually we had to speak to Burger to ask whether he could be taken to the hospital. Otherwise, he might die, we pointed out. Burger went off to confer with Chief.

Nearly an hour later, he was back. 'We have spoken to the UN people. They can take away the passenger who is ill.' Khurana was first taken to an airport hospital. Later, he was taken by the UN people to Islamabad and then flown to India.

Brara continued to lie on the seat in obvious discomfort.

'What's the problem?' I asked him.

'I probably have stomach cancer,' he said.

'That's terrible. Have you been treated?'

'I need more tests. And I am stuck here.'

By evening, the hijackers were beginning to relax. There were the beginnings of locker-room talk. 'Calcutta girls are very pretty,' Burger told me. I didn't ask how he knew. He had already talked about Mumbai. 'Full of Marathi-speaking people,' he complained. He also said he had been in Kathmandu for six months. 'I did a lot of trekking. I even went up where there was a lot of snow.'

'You're so well-travelled. You know so much about the world. Where are you from?'

He thought for a few seconds. '*Aap ye baat ko choriye.* (Let's not discuss this.)' His guard had snapped back into place.

I tried again. 'Are you from Srinagar?'

'No, no, I am Hindustani,' he said.

'When were you in Mumbai?'

'I have lived there for two or three months.'

I tried to get him to talk about Srinagar. 'It is such a lovely city. Dal Lake and the beautiful light-and-sound shows at the Dilshad Gardens.'

But he was wary. 'It isn't as lovely anymore.'

'Why is there so much terrorist activity in Srinagar these days?'

'Oh, this is the winter, you see. The fighters come down from the mountains to the city in the winter. It's so cold.'

Burger said that the ATC had told them about the arrival of a team of engineers from Kabul. 'Please come with us. Tell them what the problems with the plane are.'

I was apprehensive. If they realized we had tampered with the fuel setting, they could easily repair it. We would have to fly again.

Burger and Shankar escorted Mr Jaggia and me out of the plane, revolvers pointed to our heads. I looked at the engineers; they were tall, impressively bearded but casually dressed. They didn't look like engineers; they didn't seem to know much about the A300.

'You have to check the wings,' I said.

'We haven't been trained for that,' one of them said. Instead, they started trying to refuel the plane. All the high-octane fuel gushed out, spilling out on the tarmac. It was early evening and very chilly, the wind cutting into us as we stood there. But we were quite relieved, almost happy. They had failed to refuel the plane; we would remain in Kandahar. They couldn't make us fly somewhere worse. The UN team, I learnt, had also gone back.

There was no dinner that night. Instead, there was shairi. 'How many of you know Urdu couplets?' Burger asked unexpectedly.

'*Aap sunaiye* (You tell us),' the passengers said.

He came up with a few, and then asked the passengers for their contributions. 'Tell me some jokes,' he demanded.

The passengers asked him to tell them one or two first. He bawled them out, using his red megaphone. 'There was a plane flying,' he began. 'And then it crashes. Only a monkey survives. After the monkey is rescued, it is asked: "When the plane went down, what was the pilot doing?" "Sleeping," the monkey says. "What about the co-pilot?" it is asked. "Also sleeping." "And the air hostesses?" "Doing their make-up." "What were you doing?" the monkey is asked. "Flying the plane."'

Everyone smiled tightly. Burger demanded that Mr Jaggia come up with a joke. After the flight engineer, it was my turn. I told them a joke about socks. 'A Sardarji bought two pairs of socks, a black pair and a white pair. When he gets to office, he's wearing a mismatched pair, white sock in his left foot, black sock in his right. Then, when his peon points out the error, he expresses surprise. "There is a similar mismatched pair at home," he says.'

I told them another one. 'A man was flying with his pet parrot. When the air hostess comes to see him, the parrot kisses her. The man follows suit. When the air hostess complains, the captain of the plane orders them to be thrown out of the aircraft. When they are thrown out, the parrot asks his master. "Can you fly?" When the man shakes his head, the parrot retorts: "Why did you follow in my footsteps?"'

Then it was time to say good night. It wasn't going to be a calm night. Mr Jaggia and I were woken up in the middle of the night. We were sitting together in the front rows of the economy class. 'The sanitation people have come. They want to clean the toilets. You must show them how.'

It was bitterly cold when Burger took Mr Jaggia outside to supervise the sanitation staff. As they poured water into the tanks, a lot of it fell on Mr Jaggia. He started shivering in the freezing air, so Burger offered him his thick black jacket, ample protection against the cold.

'You're like my father. Please wear my jacket,' Burger said.

'No, I won't,' Mr Jaggia refused. 'If you think I am like your father, you're my son. How can a father watch his son freeze?'

A Toyota was parked close by. Burger pushed him into the jeep and put on the heater. The flight engineer sat there till the servicing was over. Then they came back to the plane. Mr Jaggia was still shivering when he sat next to me. He told me what had happened, and that they had wanted a bag retrieved from the hold.

Burger came to us again. He wanted us to sleep in the executive class, lying down on the seats.

'My passengers sleep sitting next to each other in the economy class. I'll stay with them,' I replied.

He tried very hard to persuade me. 'You have to be fit to fly. We want you to be in good shape.' But I simply refused.

In New Delhi, the passengers' families had waited for forty-eight hours. Storming in during a press conference which Jaswant Singh was holding at Shastri Bhavan, they said they wanted action and now. No more 'pompous statements about greatness' and 'inaction because of an ego problem' the passengers' relatives said to the press but negotiations with the hijackers towards the immediate release of passengers. As Dr Sanjeev Chibber, their spokesman said, 'The government can release one militant [Maulana Masood Azhar] for 161 passengers if they released seven for Rubaiya Sayeed [Home Minister Mufti Muhammed Sayeed's daughter] in 1989.' Pacifying the relatives, the minister admitted there was a communication gap and met some relatives in the External Affairs Ministry spokesperson's room. As a concession, the Ministries of Civil Aviation and External Affairs arranged a daily briefing for the families at the Centaur Hotel. This gesture was both too little and too late as the families had already been alienated and were very critical of the actions the government was taking.

There was trouble within the government as well. The railway minister, Mamata Banerjee, criticized government inaction at the cabinet meeting in South Block. The urban development minister, Jagmohan, first raised the issue, speaking of the failure to mount an operation at Amritsar. Then Mamata Banerjee joined in. The government was too lethargic, she said, and felt that senior ministers and bureaucrats should go to Kandahar to negotiate directly with the hijackers and rescue the passengers and crew. If no one else would go, she would, before the hijackers ordered the plane elsewhere. She said she should be accompanied by members of the Red Cross, the National Human

Rights Commission and the Minorities Commission. She also demanded that the government ask other countries to pressure the Taliban into releasing passengers. They too have citizens on board, she pointed out.

There were faint rumbles at the meeting of the three chiefs of the defense forces, General V.P. Malik, Admiral Sushil Kumar, and Air Chief Marshal A.Y. Tipnis. The armed forces were not part of the CMG. Perhaps the military could have ensured that Captain Sharan's plane never left Amritsar. Even if the commandos couldn't reach Raja Sansi Airport on time, the Army and the Air Force could have helped. There were other options, including blocking the runway and immobilizing the plane, which were never considered. In future, the chiefs felt, the government should include the defense forces in the national crisis management apparatus. In Kandahar, UN representative Erick de Mul met the Taliban and asked for the release of women and children, but without much success. Instead, he was forced to listen to the stories of human rights abuses of the people of Jammu and Kashmir. In New Delhi, Prime Minister Vajpayee ruled out granting recognition to the Taliban government just for the sake of these negotiations. The Taliban foreign minister was also threatening to 'expel' the plane if India and the UN didn't move quickly enough. With pressure and tension mounting rapidly on all sides, the Indian government seemed to be fast running out of options. There was perhaps no other way now: India would have to speak with the Taliban, a government it didn't recognize, a government that looked the other way as 'Afghan warriors' entered Jammu and Kashmir as 'freedom fighters'.

The Indo-Pak saber-rattling continued. While Jaswant Singh hinted at a Pakistani hand, his counterpart in Islamabad spoke of the hijacking as an Indian plot. The Pakistanis had 'proof of a RAW agent being on the plane.'

In Kot Bhalwal Jail, Jammu, the ring around Maulana Masood Azhar was tightened. India was keen to hear what a retired schoolteacher in Bahawalpur, a little town in Pakistan, had to say about the hijacking. The man was Allah Baksh Sabir, the father of the Maulana and Chief. 'We have nothing to do with the hijacking. We condemn it,' he is reported to have said.

Chapter Seven

Kandahar

27 December 1999

In the early hours of the morning, it must have been about 2 a.m. When Shankar woke us up. Most of the hijackers stayed awake at night, except Chief who rested. The others occasionally took turns, but mostly sat up in separate parts of the plane. I wondered how long they could last without sleep. Now Shankar wanted Mr Jaggia.

'Engineer sahab, Shankar will escort you out. We want our bag from the hold,' Chief said.

'I can't get your bag out!' the flight engineer replied.

'We have spoken to the ATC. He will help you.'

Unwillingly, Mr Jaggia went back into the cold, a knife-wielding Shankar behind him. We had checked the trim sheets, which show the load distribution of the plane—where the passengers are, how much luggage there is and in which part of the hold. We tried to locate the hijackers' bag the previous day and we found that most of the baggage was in the rear hold.

On the tarmac, Afghan engineers were waiting. They opened the cargo hold and found a container. They couldn't open it at first, then Shankar used his knife. It was an impressive knife, sharp, of course, and shiny. You could cut open an animal and, surely a man, effortlessly with it. The hijackers said the bag contained medicines and their clothes. It was dark grey and looked like a golf bag. I was fully awake while this was happening. I could hear the noise outside. I waited for the flight engineer to return. He came and sat down next to me. We talked for a while before we fell asleep.

When I woke up at 7.30 a.m. IST, I saw that Burger was carrying a different pistol. He was fiddling with it, trying to make the passengers aware that the hijackers now had some more weapons. He was also carrying a grenade I hadn't seen before. I concluded that these had come out of the bag in the hold.

I walked into the cockpit. There were two or three pistols and about a hundred loose bullets lying on the pedestal, which is just below the central instrument panel, between the pilot's and the co-pilot's seats. I also spotted four or five yellow hand grenades. I was looking for the golf bag, but it seemed to have disappeared, though I did see a new briefcase and a walkie-talkie. All these could not have fitted into a bag! I wondered where all these came from. I was very worried.

'Go back,' said Bhola, who was sitting there.

In the cabin, Burger ordered Kalpana to make tea, but only for the hijackers and the crew.

'What about the passengers?' I protested.

'It's not possible.'

'Is anything going to happen?' one of the passengers asked.

'Yes,' I said, trying to be optimistic. 'The Indian negotiating team will arrive today. We'll probably be home tonight, sleeping in our beds, and all this will be a nightmare we'll soon forget.' This was the answer I gave to all who asked me.

Samant Brara's condition was noticeably worse that morning. Several hours later, just before noon, I spoke to Burger about this.

Brara was sent off to the hospital. He was back two hours later, happier to be with his friends rather than in a freezing hospital with no medicines. 'It was so cold, and I was so uncomfortable that I told them I wanted to come back. They dropped me off.'

There we were, 160-odd people packed into a large cigar-shaped cabin for days, held hostage by five armed men. We were learning to communicate with each other. I was making friends.

In the confusion of Dubai, families had gotten separated—husbands from wives, mothers from their children. There was a temporary orphan near my seat; the mother had gotten off at Dubai.

'I am a doctor,' a man said, introducing himself. His son was with him. 'My ex-wife was an air hostess.' He told me her name. I had met her several times.

'Yes, yes, I know about you. You're the neurosurgeon. Your marriage broke up because your wife was having an affair with a flight purser,' I said. When you're all in it together, when your life is in danger, I guess you can talk about these things.

These were the only two children remaining on board, the others had been released in Dubai. The neurosurgeon's son would eat only bananas. We had to try and find him bananas every day. Both children seemed to be relatively unaffected by the prevailing tension.

'How was your son left behind?' I asked the father. 'Why didn't he get off at Dubai?'

'I thought people were being taken off to be killed. I never imagined they would return safely to New Delhi. So, I hid him under the blanket.'

I once asked Chief if the children could be released. He refused. 'We released the people when we had to.'

Another passenger, I think it was Anup Sharma, kept saying his wife would be very worried. That made me think about Navneet. If anything happened to me, she would have to look after the children. I hoped our finances were in order and that she knew where my life insurance policy was.

Breakfast and lunch passed routinely. The hours dragged on slowly. That afternoon, there was another alert.

'Heads down, heads down,' the hijackers shouted. They were more stressed and panic-stricken than they had been since we had reached Kandahar. Chief summoned me to the cockpit. Walking through the cabin, I noticed they had tied up two men in the executive class with rope. I hadn't seen them being taken there because I had been sitting in the rear of the cabin. Both were silently weeping.

When I got to the cockpit and looked outside, I saw troops surrounding the aircraft. They were Afghan commandos carrying rifles. All the shutters on the windows in the cabin were down, but from the cockpit, you could see not just the immediate surroundings full of uncertainty and squalor, but also the desolate hills of Kandahar, the sunshine, and the open sky beyond.

'Tell the ATC that if they don't remove the commandos, we'll start killing the passengers,' Chief commanded.

I got on the line to the ATC. 'The hijackers have tied up two people. I think they are going to kill them.'

I was told the deadline was noon. The hijackers were very jumpy. There was no sign of the commandos being withdrawn.

'Tell them again,' Chief said.

When I contacted the ATC again, he said the commandos were there to ensure the safety of the passengers. 'If the hijackers try something, *hum humla kar denge* (we will attack),' he said.

This made Chief finally relent. 'Okay, tell them to remove the commandos. We'll untie the two passengers.'

Burger, gun in hand, was completely on the edge. 'See, Captain sahab, they're coming, they're coming,' he would say if the commandos took even a step forward. Sometimes he would rush back to the cabin just to see if more commandos were readying to storm the plane from some other direction. The remaining three hijackers were in the cabin, but no longer watching the passengers with a hawk's eye. They were too preoccupied with the presence of the commandos. Even confined to their seats with the windows closed, the passengers sensed something was happening outside.

Shifting from the flight engineer's to the co-pilot's seat, which allowed me a better view, I watched with mounting excitement as the commandos inched closer. I thought they would storm the plane. Yes, a few people perhaps could be killed or injured in the fighting. But the rest would be rescued, and all the hijackers shot dead or captured. Even death seemed preferable to waiting in crippling uncertainty.

Chief asked me to contact the ATC again.

'The hijackers are getting very nervous. Please ask the commandos to move away. They have promised not to hurt the passengers,' I said.

'We want proof,' the ATC said.

Doctor came into the cockpit. 'I have untied the two passengers. They have gone back to their seats,' he said.

Within a few minutes, the commandos moved away, and I went back to the cabin. I saw that the two passengers who had been tied up were still in shock. They were crying; still afraid they would be killed. Just then, Burger strode in from the cockpit.

'You've done them so much harm. At least apologize to them!' I said.

Burger had a smattering of English, but the passengers did not speak the language. I called Roberto, who spoke both English and French. 'Please don't worry. We are on your side. No one's going to do anything. You're safe,' he told them. Reassured, they finally stopped weeping.

'What's happening? Are we safe?' some of the passengers around me asked. Quietly, I told them about the plane being surrounded by commandos and the panic among the hijackers.

'But they have moved back,' I said. 'The hijackers had set a deadline and the Indian government hadn't complied with their wishes. So, they threatened to kill two passengers. But they stopped after the commandos moved in.'

There was nothing more troubling than all this talk of killing passengers. We didn't want to just sit around after the hijackers started killing passengers one by one. They had already begun threatening to do so. This was also a time the hijackers allowed me to sit with passengers, interact with them. I realized that I had to help get as many of the passengers out if the shooting started. So, I would sit next to one of the doors, explain to some of them how it opened, what to do if there was an emergency. If they began shooting, escape was an option, the only option. I was careful though; I'd speak with the passenger first, find out a little about him. I was a little apprehensive, and who wouldn't be, because I thought the hijackers had a B-team, another two or three still pretending they were passengers, silently sitting with them, trying to find out what everyone was thinking. And they'd be ready to take over in case something happened to the hijackers.

So, there was the plan, amorphous, but still a plan, a 'let's try and hope for the best' one, a plan to catch the hijackers off-guard, a plan that would ensure that at least most of the passengers, though perhaps not the crew, would escape.

Saibal Kar had a similar story. 'One of the airhostesses came up to me, whispered in Bengali. This was on the third day. She said, "We will open the door in the evening, around 8.30 or 9.00 p.m. (that was the time the hijackers gathered in the business class and took it easy for a while) and all of you will slide down the chutes, and just run. I'll come with water for the passengers. There will be a lot of firing, both inside and outside (she realized that the Taliban would be supporting the hijackers), *amra shobai morey jabo* (we'll all die), but most of you will be able to slip out; you'll escape." It was winter, it got dark very early, even by 5.30 p.m. and we'd have a ghost of a chance.'

Sanjeev Sharma, who had gone outside to organize insulin injections for his cousin, had said the same thing to Kar. The Taliban were hand in glove with the hijackers. '*Bahar jakey bhag bhi gaye, bachenge nahin, maar diye jayenge. Yeh sarey miley hue hain*. (Even if you manage to get out of the plane, you'll be hunted down. They are working together.)'

'Roberto (one of the passengers the hijackers had moved up to near the wing and above where the fuel tanks were) came over. He printed currency notes for major countries, something the hijackers never knew. He and Christina, his young girlfriend, were returning from a holiday in Nepal. He too told me he knew. Once that happened, he said, the hijackers would come out, guns blazing. He'd certainly die, sitting where he was. He asked me to look after Christina. Roberto said, "Grab her hand, slide out and run for it." That was the plan,' Kar said.

The passengers didn't have a chance. That evening, the hijackers were more on their guard than ever. 'Just around 8.30, they were in their monkey caps, waving their knives and pistols, walking up and down the aisle. How they sensed what we were planning, if they did, we'll never know,' said Kar.

The passengers were quiet, except one young man. He was thin and looked exceedingly frightened. He was sitting beside Sanjeev Sharma.

'Why aren't you releasing us? It is your responsibility,' he said, raising his voice.

I motioned him to be silent. 'If you make a fuss, you'll be killed. And so will some others. Shut up,' I told him. I had noticed him before. He was openly defiant. I thought this was asking for trouble.

'Captain, remove him from here,' Sharma told me. 'He will die, and I'll also get killed.'

I told him to sit right at the end, in the last row and keep very, very quiet. But he came and sat right behind me. No other passenger wanted to sit with him.

It was past noon by now and Burger's mood was brightening after the morning's heroics. Brunch arrived. 'Ladies and gentlemen, what can I offer you?' he joked.

'Whatever there is,' a few passengers murmured.

Again, there was the now familiar Kabuli pulao. Just yellow rice with a few raisins on top.

'Today, the air hostesses won't serve any food. I need four volunteers,' Burger announced. I stood up.

'That's right, the crew needs rest,' I said.

There were a lot of volunteers. Four were chosen. This was a bit of national integration happening: two were North Indians, the other two from the South. At least, there was enough food today.

After lunch, Burger began cracking the whip about cleanliness. 'Don't drop anything on the floor and if your things are lying around, pick them up,' he said. 'An air hostess will be coming around. Put all the garbage into the polythene bag.'

All the garbage was later taken out. The people who brought the food took the garbage bags away. But this seemed futile, given the overpowering stench from the toilets, which had been there from the third day.

Passengers Rakesh and Puja Kataria remember another side of Burger. They were married on 13 December, and Puja's birthday was on 27 December. 'I am not sure how they found out, but he presented me with a shawl and some chocolate,' she said.

It was a time of impatience.

'Captain, *India se koi aya*? (Has anyone come from India?)'

No one had yet. Everyone was abusing the Indian government.

'They want to kill us here, in Kandahar,' one passenger said.

'The government doesn't care about us,' another agreed.

I knew it would take time. Hard decisions would have to be taken. Even permission from Pakistan for overflight facilities would be necessary. Such permission is necessary for a special flight over another country, especially one relating to a sensitive issue like hijacking. It would be even trickier considering that the country concerned was Pakistan.

I didn't even try to explain to the passengers, they were so angry. I thought if I tried to argue with them, they would get angry with me. And we needed desperately to work together, to cooperate with each other. So, I agreed with them, nodding away. 'Yes, yes,' I said, 'the government is taking too much time.'

One of the voices of calm was Roberto. During a lull, he strolled over.

'Can anything be done?' he asked.

'Nothing right now. What aircraft do you fly?' I asked him.

He wouldn't tell me. Instead, he brought his young girlfriend over and sat down next to me. I told him about the commandos. Later he told a few of his friends about the incident in French.

There was a woman, Canadian, I think, who was very angry with me. 'Why do you smile when you speak to the hijackers? They want to kill you, and you laugh and joke with them?' she asked.

'We don't want conflict. I am trying to build up some sort of rapport with them. If they want to kill us tomorrow, they'll think twice about it,' I explained. This was the diplomacy of the besieged, but I don't think she was convinced.

There was another woman, an American called Jeanne Moore, and more patient than the Canadian woman. And she marveled at our patience. 'If you were American, we would all be dead. You guys are so patient and nice to the hijackers!'

That evening, I saw Burger prowling around the cabin with night-vision binoculars, which I had never seen him carry before. Every so often, he looked outside to see if the commandos were inching closer.

Some time later, I could hear a plane landing. I thought, from the sound, that it was an A320. I couldn't see it, but I knew it was an Indian plane.

I turned to the flight engineer, and we shook hands.

'Our aircraft has arrived.'

'*Kya hua*? (What happened?)' asked a passenger, seeing us shaking hands. I told him.

Burger came up to us immediately after this. 'An Indian aircraft has arrived. Lee's see what happens,' he said.

We thought deliverance was at hand. That there would be discussions for an hour and then we would all go home. An hour passed as we sat waiting in the darkened cabin, expectantly.

There was a great sense of suppressed excitement. Two hours passed. At about 9.30 p.m., dinner arrived in the distinctive Indian Airlines trolleys. We were even more optimistic. Okay, I thought, the food must have arrived from India. Our last supper on the plane and it would be a memorable one. I also imagined that perhaps Indian commandos would be coming in with the trolleys. By this time, we were feverishly imagining opportunities for rescue every other second.

But disappointment was in store when we uncovered the trays. It was the same rotis and chicken or duck with green chilies. And some shrunken oranges. I learnt later the hijackers had specified that only Afghan food would be served. Who knows what they thought? Maybe that the Indian food would have powerful sleeping pills to make them drowsy and then a commando operation would be launched?

We waited till midnight, expecting a message to arrive any moment. Whenever any of the hijackers appeared, we looked up expectantly. But none of them said anything.

The passengers were constantly questioning me. 'Why don't you go and speak to the Indian contingent and have us freed? It is your responsibility,' one of them said.

All the passengers seemed happier. Maybe it was just the sight of Indian Airlines written on the trolleys. Or maybe, it was because the toilets had been cleaned, though not properly. They were joking, exchanging couplets. Everyone slept late, happy that their days of captivity would be over soon.

The hijackers were extraordinarily wary that night. They walked around on tiptoe, looking out of the window every few minutes. I am sure they were expecting a commando operation. None of them slept; neither did many of the passengers whom I had taken into confidence. In our little world, we were expecting World War III. The minutes crept by with extraordinary slowness.

When I finally slept that night, it was with a disquieting thought. There was something which had bothered me for the last two days. I had noticed something tied to Chief's wrist. Later I saw that Bhola and Doctor wore something similar around their necks, the others tied to their wrists.

When I had asked Chief what it was, he had merely said it wasn't my business. Finally, I asked Burger.

'That is our last resort. If we need it.'

I realized they were cyanide pills. I wondered what they would do before they were forced to take them.

What could the government do? 'For a couple of days,' Mansingh remembered, 'there was nothing.' If the Vajpayee government had a blind spot, it was Afghanistan, run by the Taliban. 'We had no contacts in Afghanistan, a government India hadn't recognized,' said Mansingh. India asked the UAE to help and the UN. Kofi Annan, then secretary general, had sent a team to Kandahar, but India wanted to be involved, not to leave it to the UN. 'Demonstrations outside the prime minister's house had begun and it was unnerving,' acknowledged Mansingh. 'Within the government there were differing views: one group wanted tough action, the other wanted to negotiate. I spoke with Brajesh Mishra and people from RAW and the NSG. Advani came to a CMG meeting, but there was still confusion.'

In New Delhi, as the team of Indian negotiators led by Vivek Katju, joint secretary of the external affairs ministry, flew to Kandahar, there were hopes of a quick breakthrough. With him came Ajit Doval of the Intelligence Bureau (appointed National Security Advisor in 2014), Nehchal Sandhu (later deputy National Security Advisor) and C.D. Sahay (later RAW chief). A.R. Ghanshyam, commercial counsellor of the Indian Embassy at Islamabad, had reached Kandahar in the morning to find out what the hijackers' demands were and whether they were amenable to discussion. He spoke with Chief from the control tower, but failed to make much headway. India wasn't just up against five hijackers, trained and armed by Pakistan, of course, but more stealthily, the Taliban. They wouldn't pressure the hijackers to release the passengers, even the women and children. They wouldn't allow foreign soldiers to operate in Afghanistan. So, there couldn't be a rescue operation by Indian commandos who wouldn't even be allowed to get off the plane. Nor would the Taliban use its own soldiers against the hijackers. They lacked, the Taliban claimed, soldiers with anti-hijacking capabilities. As the Taliban later told the negotiators, this wasn't a pistol-and-grenade show; there was RDX on the plane and a veritable armory of sophisticated weapons. Instead, it ringed the aircraft with tanks and heavy weaponry to deter any Indian effort to take on the commandos.

The hijackers were inflexible. Why wouldn't they be? They had all the support they needed, not just the neighboring government on their side, but Afghanistan's ruling Taliban, who were pretending to be neutral. Ajit Doval later said that initially, the negotiators requested the hijackers to be more considerate, more understanding. Why couldn't they, as a gesture of good faith, allow the women and children to go? They'd been in Kandahar for a while, they were as inflexible as terrorists on fidayeen mission are, as comfortable as any hijacker can be. Ghanshyam, who had arrived in Kandahar from Islamabad, had told New Delhi the hijackers wanted the Maulana. Or else, they'd start killing the passengers, one by one. But soon, the hijackers were making more demands. They wanted the Maulana and militants jailed in India, all 35 of them. What else did the hijackers want? They tossed a piece of paper: Azhar, of course, 35 militants, $200 million and the body of militant leader

Sajjad Afghani. In India, the government assumed this was the hijackers' opening move.

The Indian negotiators arrived in the A320 only on the evening of the 27th. The flight hadn't taken off on time. Then the Pakistanis hadn't allowed over-flight permission till late in the afternoon, and it was dusk in Kandahar when the negotiators finally got off the plane. Besides the negotiators, there were pilots, stewards, doctors, and airline engineers to repair the hijacked plane, if necessary, and a fact that was kept concealed as far as possible: 20 commandos with anti-hijacking expertise. Among the senior airline officials were Captain Suri, Captain J.R.D. Rao, Captain R.N. Singh, Flight Engineer A.K. Nagar and Mr M. Pais.

'The negotiating team met with Mr Muttawakil, the civil aviation minister and the local corps commander. Muttawakil was always civil, but the initial demand was a maximalist one and Delhi's reaction was that it was impossible,' said Mansingh. The negotiators spoke with Muttawakil two or three times every day and Katju would brief Mansingh every evening. 'The team was told to keep talking and whittling down the demands. The Taliban officials were the go-between...we don't talk with terrorists. It wasn't possible to meet the crew or the passengers.'

All the Taliban, who were in regular touch with the Pakistanis, did was tell the hijackers not to harm the passengers. This was after they threatened to start shooting passengers if negotiations were delayed. But, of course, they wouldn't negotiate with the hijackers on India's behalf. There would be no goodwill gesture. No passengers would be released, not even women and children. Instead, there were threats of harm if negotiations were delayed. This was when the Taliban stepped in. They would not negotiate with the hijackers, but quite firmly told them that the passengers should not be harmed. Ghanshyam, who had come in a little before the negotiating team from Delhi, had initially managed to extend the tentative deadlines of the hijackers twice.

Back in Delhi, the Union Cabinet remained divided over what was to be done. Mamata Banerjee boycotted the cabinet meeting. She wanted politicians to go to Kandahar, not only bureaucrats. The Indo-Pak war of words continued. The BJP national executive reiterated what the government had said the previous day: 'Pakistan's pivotal role is evident from the main demand of the hijackers: the release of Maulana Azhar.' It wasn't just the passengers' families who were restive, Navneet Sharan was very anxious. She called Mrs Jaggia, who was crying. Her daughters were also in tears. They were afraid the whole episode could only end badly.

'Everything would be all right,' Mrs Sharan tried to reassure her. 'I am very confident. Your husband and mine will both return.' But she wasn't feeling that confident at all.

'I called Anil Sharma's wife Simi. She was crying as well. That really shook me up. I thought I was the one who needed reassurance and everyone I called was crying.'

Shaken, she decided to call Sharad Yadav. 'What are you doing for us?' she asked.

'Yes, you brought back some passengers from Dubai. You spoke of the safe release of passengers, but you haven't said a thing about the safe release of the crew, and you are the civil aviation minister!'

Mrs Sharan also called Jaswant Singh. 'He came on the line but was very tense. I asked him what he was doing to free the passengers and crew. Why, I asked, was the government waiting for the all-party meeting before doing anything?'

'We are doing everything possible and everything necessary to get everyone back,' the external affairs minister replied.

Finally, she called the prime minister.

'My husband is a fan of yours, but I never liked the BJP. I can't understand why he is your fan,' she said as the prime minister listened patiently. She reminded him that five or six extremists had been freed to secure the release of Rubaiya Sayeed. Were 162 people not the equal of one girl? She said that she hoped to be born into a politician's family in her next life so that they would receive similar support in times of crisis.

'*Hum poori koshish kar rahe hain* (We are doing our best),' the prime minister replied.

'Sir, I want to meet you. Please let me know where and when.'

'Okay. At my residence. At 4 p.m.'

Mrs Sharan and families of the crew reached the prime minister's office that evening at about 4.30 p.m. The change in the time and venue was made at the intervention of a union minister from Andhra Pradesh. The prime minister's principal secretary and national security advisor, Brajesh Mishra, and Vasundhara Raje Scindia, the union minister of state for personnel, were there. They all stood up when the prime minister entered.

The meeting began on a strangely abrupt note. 'I am sorry we are meeting like this,' the prime minister said. Then he added, 'Other nations are trying to help us.'

Mrs Sharan was stressed, and hence uncharacteristically combative. 'But what are you doing?' she asked.

'The Indian ambassador to Islamabad has gone to Kandahar to assess the situation,' the prime minister said.

'Assess what? It is -10°C in Kandahar.'

'Madam, please be quiet,' Mr Mishra intervened.

'This is the continuation of Kargil. This is the second episode,' the prime minister said.

'I don't think the two can be co-related...' Mrs Sharan replied.

'Think of the widows of Kargil,' the prime minister said. All this reminder served to achieve was that it made everyone more apprehensive. Was he preparing everyone for the worst, they wondered.

'Sir, one last thing,' Mrs Sharan said. 'Do we have your assurance that everyone will be safe?'

'*Achcha, mere ko phansi de dena* (Okay, you can hang me then),' the prime minister said.

'Sir, this will be a *phansi* for the hostages and their families.'

When the prime minister left, Ms Scindia asked Mrs Sharan if she would speak with the passengers' families. 'We need your help. We want you to meet the passengers.'

That evening she went to meet the passengers' families. They were in worse shape than she was. They had no news. She, of course, had only the same meagre information as they did but she felt that as the commander's wife, she had to set an example of courage. This helped her maintain her fortitude.

'Are the passengers getting anything to eat? Have you spoken with your husband?' someone asked.

'Have you eaten today?' Mrs Sharan asked. He hadn't.

Nor had many others.

'If you haven't eaten, don't worry about them. They will be all right. My husband will bring everyone back,' she asserted confidently.

Chapter Eight

Kandahar

28 December 1999

'Something will happen today,' I told myself as I awoke, bleary-eyed after an uncomfortable night. It was still dark. I had slept fitfully. And the morning began badly.

'Can I have some tea?' I asked Kobita Mukherjee.

'No, sir,' was the reply. 'There is no water.'

'Okay, we have cans of soda. Open them, let the carbon dioxide fizz out and boil the water.'

That's what she did. But the hot jug in the galley wasn't working so the air hostesses heated the cans directly on the oven. As I sipped tea, I realized how miserable the passengers must be. They had been given nothing to drink that morning. There was no water, only three or four cans of soda. The only water arrived at 4 p.m. My throat was dry through the day. I had only a few gulps of soda. Everyone was clamoring for water, especially the children. There was none. In desperation, I walked into the cockpit around 11 a.m.

'There are only a few cans of beer left. The children are crying for water; let's serve them beer for the moment,' I said. 'At least, they won't get dehydrated.'

'Okay, go ahead,' Chief agreed reluctantly.

I felt saddened and guilty that I could only offer beer to the children. As I walked to the toilet at the end of the cabin, passengers were ready with questions. They tugged at my trousers to stop me. 'Did anything happen last night? Is there any hope?' someone asked.

I noticed they were looking at me with hope. And I could only be impatient with them. I didn't know the answers. 'I spent the night with you, in the plane. How will I know?' I asked.

The toilet was very messy. If one went in, one's clothes would be stinking for about ten minutes after that. Things were that bad.

Later that morning, Chief came up and asked me, 'Do you know what happened in New Delhi today?'

'How would I know? I was in the cabin.'

'The police are lathi-charging the relatives of passengers. And the relatives are heckling senior members of the Union Cabinet, including the external affairs minister Jaswant Singh.'

He probably thought I would feel very despondent; I felt quite relieved. At least, there's some pressure on the government. Something will happen, I thought.

I wanted to share this information with the passengers. I used the public address system. 'Your relatives are pressuring the government. I am certain things are moving. Maybe today… Freedom is coming.'

But before that happened, there was much more suffering in store for us. The auxiliary power unit (APU) in the plane, which provided us the air conditioning and heating, broke down. The plane's batteries had run out. I spoke to the ATC on a walkie-talkie borrowed from the airport authorities. The hijackers had another one too.

'Can you send us another battery?' I asked the ATC. They complied several hours later, and we started up the APU. There was a sigh of relief when the lights came back, but our minds were elsewhere. What were our negotiators doing? Why were they taking so long? When would we be released? No one had any answers.

There was no water, but there was breakfast: a sort of omelet, oily but it was food. There was nothing for the vegetarians. I felt terrible, but what use was that.

I decided to ask the passengers. 'Do you have anything to eat? Do any of you have anything in your bags that you can share with the passengers who have no breakfast?'

A few passengers volunteered. One by one, they walked to the executive class where their hand baggage was. There wasn't much, but there was something, a packet or two of biscuits and a few pastries.

It was time to plead with the hijackers for water. 'It will come,' said Doctor.

Burger had an alternative. 'Take Allah's name. Repeat after me.'

I am not sure what it was, but it appeared to be a form of namaz.

'*Allah, hamare upar karam karo*. (God, protect us.) Allah, please give us strength and send us home safely. Allah, save us.'

Everyone joined in, sitting in their seats, arms raised. And almost everyone was doing that only because they were being forced to. They wanted to be on Burger's good side.

I did the same thing.

Later I talked to Rajinder and Mr Jaggia. 'What will you do if we go back safely?' I asked Rajinder.

'Don't talk of these things. Let's leave first. We're still sitting here.' He seemed very depressed.

Mr Jaggia asked me what I would do.

'I am not sure. I know I'll be very happy if everyone goes back.'

There was a Japanese woman on the flight, in her early thirties and unmarried. I think her name was Chiaki Hisada. I have never met someone so optimistic. She woke up every morning at 7 a.m. and got ready. It's strange what we remember about people. I remember her alarm clock, small and pink. She set her alarm every two hours and she would eat something, either whatever she had in her bag or what was served. She was very charming, and she seemed to shut out all her miseries. She wore beautiful clothes, freshened up every day and behaved with such quiet dignity. It didn't seem from her behavior that she was a hostage on a hijacked plane in an alien inhospitable land, in the hands of five armed rogues. She taught me a lot. Someone who could seem so happy and so optimistic in such adversity deserves admiration. She used to take permission from the hijackers to smoke. When this was refused, she would go into the toilet and smoke.

Finally, Shankar couldn't take her politeness anymore. 'Okay, smoke here,' he said, pointing towards the rear galley. 'But don't smoke in the toilet.' She paved the way for the other smokers on the plane. When they saw her smoke in the rear galley, they knew where to congregate. The floor was full of cigarette butts and the stale smell of cigarette smoke was everywhere.

Even in these difficult moments, there was occasional laughter. In the early afternoon, Burger was talking to Kobita and Kalpana in the middle galley. 'Women from Calcutta are beautiful,' he said. As he was walking away, one of them said, 'We are beautiful, but we are tired!'

I couldn't help but laugh. I walked up to Burger. 'Can't you see how attractive all our air hostesses are?'

He got the point. 'No, no. You're all very beautiful,' he told them.

Dr Anita Joshi, one of the passengers, had been looking after the passengers who were wounded or ill right from Christmas Day. Then, she couldn't take it anymore. She had something like a nervous breakdown. The tension was beginning to get to everyone, and it was clear she had problems. We had to calm her down, bring her back to a level of normalcy. Only God knew how much longer we would be on the plane. I massaged her hands and feet and took her to Chief.

'Please allow her to sit in the cockpit. I want her to get some fresh air,' I told him. There wasn't much else I could do. I opened the window. She felt a little better after that, but not much. She didn't walk around as much as she used to and couldn't continue helping those who felt ill as tirelessly as she had done before.

There was another passenger, an elderly man. I think he had an alcohol problem. And that day, he approached Shankar. He needed his rum ration from his bag. The euphemism he used was supari.

'There is some supari in my bag. Can I get some of the stuff out?'

He opened his bag and took out a quart bottle. He walked straight to the rear galley and found himself a tumbler. Pouring some rum from the bottle, he swigged down a couple of pegs neat.

Shankar pointed this out to me. 'Do you know what he just did?'

'Let him be. He's an elderly man. We can forgive him his alcoholism,' I said, after Shankar told me the story. But he really did like supari as well. He used to sit at the back and crack betel nuts with a nutcracker. I told him not to.

'The hijackers will kill you if they saw you with the nutcracker,' I said. But he wasn't bothered. He continue cracking his supari even while I was telling him not to. This was also a day for faked illnesses. The people doing this hoped desperately that the hijackers would release them or at least send them to a hospital. Anything to get out of the plane! They remembered that Khurana and Brara had been allowed out of the plane. We had been in the plane for over a hundred hours by now. A newly married man pretended he was having a fit. I was certain he was faking it, and I could only feel sorry for his wife. She was crying.

'Did you know he is epileptic?' I asked her.

'No, no. I had no idea,' she said.

It was my duty to play nurse. I duly massaged his feet, and soon realized how good an actor he was. There were a few others as well who pretended to be ill. Some complained of heart ailments. Others pretended to faint. I had only one cure for them: persuasion. I told them to cut out the dramatics. I had asked Chief. And he, in no uncertain terms, announced that no one would be allowed to go.

'If they die, they die on the plane. If they live, they live,' he declared.

That afternoon there was more Kabuli pulao in aluminum containers, the now familiar brown rice with a sprinkling of raisins on top. An hour later, at 4 p.m., we had fresh supplies of drinking water, and I saw the smiles come back and the sighs of relief. There were about fifty plastic bottles, but in an hour, the water was gone. We were all so thirsty!

In the evening, Roberto and his girlfriend came and sat with us. She spent so much time talking with Mr Jaggia that I teased him a bit.

'Why are you hitting on her?' I asked.

'I am not,' he replied, flustered.

'Yes, you are.'

We were still waiting for something to happen. We wondered as we tried to go to sleep that night whether we would ever get home.

How terrible conditions were inside the A300 and how unyielding the hijackers were was seen by the world as the first photographs of Kandahar Airport arrived. As a Taliban soldier handed over a plate of rice (Burger's Kabuli pulao) to the hijackers, he had a handkerchief on his nose. The stench inside the plane was almost unbearable. And then there was the announcement of the list of the hijackers' demands.

The negotiators were getting nowhere. The early morning request for the release of Rachna Katyal was turned down. That the hijackers wouldn't release a woman married on 3 December and widowed three weeks later (and they had killed her husband) only showed how bloody-minded they were. The family had appealed to the hijackers for her release. TV channels had carried it and the negotiators said her release would be the right thing to do. In reply to the negotiators' request, the hijackers asked for time. They came back half an hour later. The answer was 'No.' Rachna Katyal could not be released. Why had they asked for time? Were they consulting others? Did they want to check with their handlers in Pakistan?

Envoys from other countries, including Switzerland, Spain, Italy, Belgium, France, Canada and Australia, were also present at the airport. But arguments that hostage taking was a crime against humanity were dismissed with the remark that the Indian government wasn't doing much for the passengers. If the demands weren't met, the passengers would be shot, the hijackers said.

What were the demands? The hijackers were sticking, almost literally, to their guns: it wasn't just the Maulana, the 35 militants considered hardcore by the Indian government, and US $200 million (860 crore rupees at the time), but also the remains of Sajjad Afghani, a militant leader killed by security forces during a jail riot in Jammu and Kashmir in 1998. He was arrested in February 1994 and moved to Tihar Jail and then to Kot Bhalwal Jail. When the Indian government looked at the names, they found they were, expectedly enough, either from Pakistan or from Pakistan-occupied Kashmir. Most of them were from the Harkat ul-Ansar. The finger of suspicion was now clearly pointing towards Pakistan and the ISI.

On Christmas Eve, Vinay Kumar, a joint secretary of the home ministry, had blamed the ISI, out of habit, it had seemed then. Now, it was all in the open.

As Jaswant Singh appealed to the international community to 'understand' the demands; a senior home ministry official dismissed them as 'obnoxious'. It was clearly the first stage only. The hijackers were expected to bargain, to come down from their original position. The prime minister met the three service chiefs; finally, the armed forces were in the picture.

Afghanistan's foreign minister, Muttawakil's statements ruled out any possibility of a rescue operation. He also ruled out granting asylum to the hijackers. 'The wish of Afghanistan is a quick resolution. The Taliban insists there should be no shedding of innocent blood.' He also suggested only the hijackers and the Indian officials could sort things out. One side had the lock, the other the key. They had to get together.

The US publicly responded to Jaswant Singh's appeal. 'Ending the hijacking without further loss of life is our goal,' said Jim Fullin, the White House national security council spokesman.

The passengers' families were growing desperate and resorted to measures that further embarrassed the government. Carrying placards, they camped outside the prime minister's Race Course Road residence. The prime minister finally agreed to meet them.

Mrs Sharan met some passengers' family members at Ms Scindia's residence and accompanied them to Race Course Road. They asked the prime minister what he was doing to ensure the release of their family members.

'We are trying our level best, but we have no direct diplomatic ties with the Taliban,' the prime minister said.

After he finished, Ms Scindia asked Mrs Sharan to speak to the passengers' relatives.

'We are in the same boat,' she said. 'I am trying to be brave because Captain Sharan is brave. He is very strong; you shouldn't worry too much. I promise you my husband will bring back everyone.'

The prime minister smiled, and some passengers' relatives clapped, but everyone wasn't pleased.

'You've changed sides. You're speaking for the government,' some family members said.

The government wanted to counteract some of the negative publicity and ensure that the pressure from the passengers' families was eased. The Surya Foundation, a BJP-backed organization, brought forward family members of Kargil martyrs to inculcate a spirit of sacrifice for the nation. Colonel V.N. Thapar (Retd.), the father of Captain Vijayant Thapar, posthumously awarded the Mahavir Chakra, made a statement.

'We sympathize with the plight of the families. We have also lost our loved ones. If we give way now that will give birth to many more incidents of terrorism,' he said.

Chapter Nine

Kandahar

29 December 1999

By now, we would wake up every morning with a familiar sense of despair. All the physical discomforts of sitting in one place, hunger, thirst, being dirty, had turned into a numb weariness. When I awoke, I had a dismal sense that this day too would be like the preceding one.

The toilets were overflowing. You could smell them from about fifteen feet with the doors closed. I was worried that now maybe people would really start falling sick. Everything took a toll: fatigue, stress, claustrophobia, the lack of proper meals and the unhygienic toilets. What would the hijackers do if there was an epidemic? Shoot us all?

Meanwhile, all we could do was wait for the two sets of negotiators, the hijackers and the Indian officials, to reach an agreement. No one told us what was going on, but I knew, or I thought I knew, how things were going. If they had gone well, the hijackers would be cheerful. They would be nice to us. If they hadn't got their way, they would be grim and irritable. At times, they would let fly at us. 'You should be ashamed of being Indian. Your government is refusing to accept our demands. Clearly, they don't want your early release. They want to kill all of you,' Burger shouted in frustration at one of the passengers.

The passengers exercised remarkable restraint and were diplomatic. One of them even said he would do something for the people of Kashmir once he was released. This could have been another manifestation of the Stockholm syndrome. But I also believe that the passengers sometimes said what they did just to keep on the right side of the hijackers. After all, everyone wanted to go home and they thought their chances of saving their lives would be greater if they were polite to the hijackers and did not unnecessarily anger them. I too used to monitor the behavior of the hijackers. I wanted to see their reactions. This could mean the difference between early release and more days in captivity, maybe between life and death.

Sometimes the hijackers threw us crumbs. We were allowed to send messages to the Indian delegates. So, the passengers wrote long letters, hoping the government would hear their pleas. There were also some letters of complaint. Their biggest problem, many said, was the toilet. The food was quite bad. Burger would read the letters before handing them over.

We wondered when the hijackers slept and where. I had begun to work that out. I noticed that only one or two slept every night. Shankar would try to stay awake every night. His eyes were swollen and red, but he was still alert.

The hijackers would take turns to roam around the aisles and two would stand guard, near the front and rear doors respectively. They had sealed off the plane, all the windows were covered with white cloth. No one could see anything happening inside the cabin.

Then there were what I called 'horror hours', the six-hour spells of keeping our heads down. If we had to go to the toilet, we would have to raise our hands and one of the hijackers would, embarrassingly, escort us. Later, towards the end of our ordeal, the hijackers allowed little comforts like smoking in our seats, and they even provided us with cigarettes at times. The little favors were rare, and no one really ever felt free. We had a treat that morning; there were lots and lots of almonds.

Of course, the passengers were completely stressed out. So were the crew. But the hijackers were also showing signs of strain. Mr Jaggia and I were sitting in the cockpit with Chief when he explained to us what a great hero his brother Maulana Masood Azhar was, how hard he had fought for the cause and how much he was suffering. I listened, sitting across him, in the metallic grey cabin full of switches. And there he was, one minute sitting and talking about his brother, and then suddenly there was a catch in his voice and he burst into tears. I couldn't even see his face, he was still wearing his monkey cap. I hadn't seen anyone sob wearing one before! And then, he hugged me and I patted him on the shoulder.

'Don't worry. Everything will be all right,' I told him. I had to, I thought. He may have been in tears, but he still had a gun. And we were still his captives.

As luck would have it, Burger walked into the already cramped cockpit right then and, seeing his boss being patted on the shoulder by me, was about to break down as well. It was Mr Jaggia who walked up to him.

'Don't be so emotional,' he said quietly. 'Everything will be okay.'

When the hijackers allowed passengers to smoke in their seats, I intervened in the interests of those who did not smoke. 'If they have to smoke, let them walk to the back of the plane and smoke near the toilets,' I told Doctor. 'Then there won't be cigarette smoke in the cabin.'

I was still the target of questions. The passengers seemed to think I was privy to information about what was happening at the negotiations. But I was as much in the dark as they were.

I had the same answer each time. 'Negotiations are going on. Don't worry, we'll all go back safely. Believe me and believe in God. Everything will be all right.' What else could I say? I would pat the more disturbed ones on their backs just to shore up confidence. Later, some passengers thanked me for my reassurances; it was all they had then. And it meant a lot to them, giving them hope.

I realized I had to keep a brave face. For the safety of the passengers, I had to appear strong even though my knees were wobbly. I tried to be confident even when I was wondering whether I would ever go home alive.

If I was trying to look after the passengers' minds and inject confidence and hope, the three doctors on the flight tried hard to ensure there were no major illnesses. Usually, we could get the basic medicines we wanted. Burger would carry a requisition slip to the Taliban people, and within an hour, we would get what we wanted.

Burger came to me. 'Do we have any napkins?'

'What do we need them for?' I asked.

He explained to me that several women were having their periods. They needed assistance.

'Why don't you just let them go?' I requested him. 'They must be uncomfortable.'

Burger refused.

I asked the air hostesses.

'Yes,' one of them said. 'We desperately need them.'

We had none in the cabin. The women had to use paper napkins at first, but the hijackers did manage to provide us with sanitary towels in a while. There was also the problem of disposal. By the evening, the toilets were clogged with used sanitary napkins. It was an indescribable mess and was becoming a health hazard. There were some napkins on the floor of the toilets, and people had menstrual blood on their shoes if they went in. Things were getting worse. I hoped desperately no one would fall seriously ill.

People began refusing to eat. They just couldn't bear going to the toilets. No one wanted to sit in the rear seats; the area was full of the stench of the overflowing toilets.

Finally, I had an idea. 'If you have bottles of perfume or deodorant with you, please pass them on to the flight purser,' I told the passengers. We had to spray the cabin just to keep the stench away. But the relief was only temporary.

The executive class was virtually a hospital. Dr Anita Joshi, one of the doctors, was ill. Claustrophobia, understandably enough, was becoming a serious problem.

Rachna Katyal had asked one of the air hostesses about her husband, Ripin. She was told that he had been released at Dubai.

Rachna came to me. 'Tell me what has happened to my husband,' she said.

'I saw him get off. I know he is safe,' I lied. I knew what had happened to him, but I wasn't sure how much longer we would be staying in the plane. A hysterical woman on the plane would be an additional problem to handle, I had decided.

I called for Burger. 'You tell her that her husband is safe, and he got off at Dubai,' I told him.

He agreed. He pointed to Rajni. 'She helped him get off the plane at Dubai,' he said.

I quietly motioned to Rajni and she nodded.

'Please take care of her. She should not know her husband is dead,' I told Rajni. Later, the air hostesses told me her hands were always cold and she would shiver in fear. Maybe she already knew or feared the worst.

Satish, our flight purser, told me another story of a passenger in discomfort. He was a heart patient and in such terrible shape that he couldn't walk. He needed to go to the toilet but couldn't get up. Satish was forced to administer an emergency bedpan, he found a used mineral water bottle. For every meal that interminable day there was the inevitable Kabuli pulao, the same brown rice and the raisins.

But there was very little of it. Fortunately, perhaps, a few people refused to eat.

'I can't bear to go to the toilet,' one passenger told me. Others were suffering from constipation, gas and acidity; even Mr Jaggia was ill.

I kept telling the crew and a few selected passengers to be prepared for any eventuality or for an emergency, a euphemism for a possible hand-to-hand fight with the hijackers if the commandos attacked. I had been thinking about it for a few days. If we fought the hijackers, many would die; perhaps, at least a hundred of us would survive. If they decided to kill us, they could slaughter each one of us!

I walked to the rear of the plane where the air hostesses were sitting. 'Prepare for an emergency,' I told them. 'If push comes to shove, just start opening the emergency chutes. We have to save as many passengers as we can.'

Rajni, one of our air hostesses, was brave. 'I am with you,' she assured me. 'I will save the passengers and if there is a fight,

I am sure we will kill at least one of the hijackers.' I asked her to spread the word. 'Please inform Anil Sharma, the other air hostesses and as many passengers as you can when you're serving them meals.'

The hijackers couldn't eat with their hoods on. They had to take them off. Three or four of them would lock the cockpit from inside and then take off their hoods to eat. But not Burger; he wasn't afraid of being identified. He would walk right down the aisle, occupy the last row and take off his hood.

'No one look back,' he declared each time.

The hijackers reserved the toilets near the cockpit, which were cleaner, only for themselves and a few passengers who were ill. The rest of us couldn't use them initially, but on 30 December, when the talks were almost over, the crew was also allowed.

Sometimes there were a few meagre comforts as well. Today, with the food, we had a gift, presumably all the way from Islamabad: cans of Coke, Pepsi and Fanta. I am quite positive there weren't that many cans in Kandahar. The Taliban could not allow or afford these emblems of so-called western economic imperialism, but they were very welcome, especially because there were enough cans for all of us.

I was worried about the passengers at night; there just were not enough blankets. Indian Airlines blankets aren't very large, so when a passenger used one, his or her upper body or legs would stick out. It was -10°C outside, and some of the passengers, who were not warmly clad, were shivering continually. For some reason, the hijackers didn't want us to sleep well. They didn't turn on the heating at night.

One of the passengers did me a favor. He had picked up some so-called Eskimo blankets from Kathmandu, and these were large and very warm. He lent them to us. I think they saved us. Mr Jaggia, Rajinder and I used to sit in the executive class seats, leaning back and as comfortable as possible, the thick yellow blankets over us.

Many passengers weren't so lucky. Sometimes when a passenger went to the toilet in the middle of the night, he would return to find his blanket had been taken away by another passenger. He wouldn't be able to find it in the dark and in any case, all Indian Airlines blankets are identical. The poor passenger would have to shiver all night.

Blankets were all the passengers were allowed to steal from each other. The hijackers took responsibility for all the hand luggage lying in the executive class. They made sure that nothing was stolen. The hijackers were also impeccably behaved with the women, whether they were passengers or crew. They were always respectful and referred to them as 'sisters'.

But their venom against India and everything Indian was enormous. As the negotiations continued, they told us that the Indian government was not really bothered about us. It had nine hundred million people to take care of. Why would it bother about a mere 160 people on a hijacked plane? They said the Indian government would let us die; the Indian delegation had only come here to buy dry fruit and was not bothered about looking after us.

That evening, Chief called me. 'It doesn't look as if the negotiations will lead anywhere,' he said. About the negotiators, he said, '*Aapko marwake chodenge*. (They will ensure that you have to die.)' They had been talking the whole day and getting nowhere. Their initial offer was this: release Maulana Masood Azhar, and fifteen passengers would be released in exchange. The next phase of the negotiations would begin after that. The negotiators refused to agree to such plans.

Chief seemed very upset; the deadlocked talks were beginning to tell on him. 'First the UN delegation came, and they did nothing for us. Then the Indian delegation arrived, and they don't even want to do anything!' he said. Chief spoke a lot about UN negligence, about how it was doing nothing to stop the massacre of the Muslims in Chechnya and in other parts of the world.

Despite the deadlock in negotiations, this was a day when lightness descended on the passengers, for all the problems with the food and the toilets and the strains of captivity. Some efforts were made by the Ariana Airlines people to clean the toilets. But we were a little relaxed. It may have come from the fact that we human beings are amazingly adaptable and so we were getting used to even this strange routine. Also, the imminence of death receded a bit, probably because of the polite behavior of the hijackers. With one exception: Bhola. The stress was telling on him. He seemed troubled. 'Keep quiet. Nobody is to speak,' he shouted suddenly at intervals. 'Nobody is to get up from his seat. I have a gun. I could shoot all of you.'

The passengers despised him. 'See how thin and weak he looks. And he's caused us the most trouble. When we kill these hijackers, he will be the first to die,' one of them told me. There seemed something very adolescent and immature about him. He did not seem to be able to communicate normally with people.

Dinner consisted of Kandahari roti and roast duck, cold and unappetizing. People ate very little. Afterwards, there was no antakshari, no couplets. We waited for the negotiators and the hijackers to arrive at a decision.

At 9 p.m., Burger arrived in the cabin. 'We have reached a decision. They're going to let one of us go. And we'll let off fifteen of the passengers,' he said.

'Which fifteen? There are over 150 people on the plane,' I said.

'The patients and a few of the women.'

He wandered among the passengers. '*Aap aage aa jaiye* (Please come forward),' he started selecting randomly. He asked the people selected to go sit in the executive class.

He selected fifteen people, including the sick passengers and the two children. There was one man the hijackers wanted off the plane. His name was Iqbal Singh, but they thought he was a Muslim. He was a tall and well-built young man, and I wanted him left on the plane. I thought he would be of immense assistance if there was an emergency where we had to try to overpower the hijackers.

'Why do they want you off the plane?' I asked him.

'They think I am Muslim. I am Sikh.'

I requested him to take the Japanese woman. When I told Burger, he refused.

'Why do you want her to leave? She looks perfectly happy here. She is the only one who appears to be unaffected by it all,' he replied.

I admired her strength and derived inspiration from it. She was so totally cool. If I joked with the passengers and even the hijackers, and tried to lighten things a bit, she was partly the reason. She made me realize that being tense would serve no purpose. It was better to appear relaxed.

The other person I spoke up for was Rachna Katyal. 'Why don't you release her?' I asked Burger. He agreed.

'Captain, I'll do it immediately.'

He brought her over to the executive class soon after. I also tried to persuade him to let off a few more. I counted the people who had been selected. There were thirty-three seats in the executive class and all of them were occupied.

Many of us, including Mr Jaggia, Rajinder and I as well as about a dozen passengers gave Dr Anita Joshi our telephone numbers and requested her to call our homes to reassure our families.

Mr Jaggia made a final request. 'Please take two more passengers. They are causing a lot of trouble.' This was just an excuse to push in as many passengers as possible in the list of those who were to be freed.

The hijackers agreed. Now, we could only wait and watch.

The passengers left behind were a little agitated. Thirty-five of their fellow sufferers were leaving for home and many of them were being left behind in Kandahar with the hijackers.

One member of the crew started crying. 'My mother is a heart patient. I want to leave,' he pleaded.

I did not approve of this attitude. He was a member of the crew. And we should be the last people to leave the plane, after every passenger had left.

'Don't expect to leave before every passenger has left. It is against the rules in any case,' I said. 'Many of the people being released are ill. The women must go. Their children have been left off. How can I keep them on the plane and let you go?'

I pointed to the air hostesses.

'Look at these girls. They have families, husbands and children. You don't even have a family. And you're crying like a woman. Shame on you.'

He was instantly remorseful. 'No, sir, I don't want to go. Please let me send a message to my parents through one of them.'

I asked for his telephone number. He gave me a letter. 'I am going to tell the negotiators from the cockpit to call your parents and tell them you are safe.'

Many of the passengers were also in tears. I tried to reassure them. 'Don't worry. We will leave too, tomorrow. I am sure everything will work out.' But it was hard to be convincing when I thought it was unlikely.

The aggressive passenger who was sitting behind me started saying he wanted to go. I tried to calm him down. 'Please sit quietly. Otherwise, you'll be in trouble, and no one will be able to save you.'

He was quiet for a bit, and again, he started crying. 'I want to go,' he kept saying. Then he started screaming. 'I want to go.'

It took a lot of effort to deal with a man who was so stressed out, especially when we were all so tense and exhausted. But I tried. 'Look, the hijackers have released people they want to release. It is up to them. The passengers I have helped are either seriously ill, or women who were separated from their children in Dubai, or very elderly. All of them have problems.'

Sanjeev Sharma spoke to me quietly, 'Captain, send him right to the back of the cabin.'

'I cannot punish him, only try to convince him and I think I have,' I said.

Sharma too complained he was ill. He sat grimacing, a hand on his heart. I called one of the doctors.

'He's largely all right. There is no heart problem. It's just that he is feeling suffocated sitting in the cabin for six days. He wants to be released,' the doctor said.

'I can't do that. At this rate, all the passengers would develop problems!'

Though many of those who were being left behind must have asked to be among the chosen thirty-five, most of them nevertheless felt happy at this turn of events. For a start there would be more space in the cabin and fewer people to share the toilets with. More than that, it was the first ray of light at the end of a pitch-dark tunnel, a talisman of hope. They felt they too would get home, perhaps not tomorrow, but maybe the day after. The hijackers were behaving better. This painful process of deciding who would go and who wouldn't took a couple of hours. It was nearly midnight by the time it was over, and I was tired. I picked up my blanket and decided to try to sleep with one eye open. The negotiations were going on. And as soon as the door opened, I would get up and help the passengers off. The plane all the passengers wanted to get on was the Indian Airlines A320 parked on the tarmac right behind our aircraft. I could see it when I went to the back of the plane to speak to Doctor. The other plane was only a thousand meters away. There were many Taliban security men on the tarmac. It was a relief just to look at it. But paradoxically, I also felt even more helpless. Here I was, stuck on this plane for days, and I couldn't do a thing about it. I could only look outside, towards the barren mountains and at the people on the tarmac. Whenever I was summoned to the cockpit, I would look outside. I spent as much time as I could in the cockpit. After five days in the cabin, the sunlight on the arid hills looked so pretty. There wasn't even a single touch of green, only brown soil and rocks, but it was still beautiful.

All these days, all I could do was spend time just talking to the hijackers, to persuade them not to kill the passengers, or to ask for smaller favors, things that would make life a little easier. Or I walked up and down the aisle, talking with passengers, trying to ensure they didn't do or say things that would anger the hijackers and make them do something violent. I kept telling the passengers: 'Whatever you do, tell me in advance.'

And all the time the pressures were building up. I was tired, very tired.

In the evening, Roberto was walking around the cabin.

I talked to him to hear his suggestions and advice. 'What do you fly these days?' I asked.

'Usually my own planes, the Falcon jets and my helicopters.' He gave me his visiting card. 'Don't tell anyone or show it to anyone,' he said. He was a president of a major corporation. He used to be a Swissair pilot, but he resigned to run the family business after his father died. I did not mention this to anyone.

I did not want the hijackers to negotiate separately with the Swiss government for his release.

The food situation was improving, or we were getting less critical. The passengers were far less finicky about meals. Even a few of the strict vegetarians were eating chicken. Quite a number were not eating at all, of course, and many were living on liquids. Sanjeev Sharma, who sat next to me, only drank orange juice. It was quite an operation, he would squeeze the shrunken oranges by hand into a cup. He too didn't want to have to go to the toilet. By now, all the passengers talked with one another.

Occasionally, they would be allowed to move around the plane and sit wherever they wanted to. For all the tension and discomfort of captivity, they were relatively relaxed. That evening, Chief called me to the cockpit once again. He habitually sat there and had begun to keep me informed about where things stood with the negotiators. He was having dinner, his hood covering his head and the upper part of his face. But his mouth and jaw could be seen.

Bhola stood up immediately. 'Don't come in. Wait for a couple of minutes.'

Chief was more welcoming. 'No, no. Come in, Captain,' he said, pulling his hood down all the way.

Chief and I had developed a working relationship. I called him Chief sahab. He called me Captain sahab. I asked him if there had been any progress. He looked very tired and depressed. He wasn't happy about the way the negotiations were going. 'We were the hijackers once. Now it appears we have been hijacked!' I could only laugh at his humor, and he joined in. 'We have seen how patient you are. If we are here for another three or four days, you'll stand before us with folded hands like our air hostesses do and say "Goodbye. We are sorry for the inconvenience." Don't you think so?' I asked him.

But the relationship with the other hijackers was not evenly smooth. Bhola was often unnecessarily aggressive, as was Shankar. The latter would swagger around the cabin, sometimes taking the pin off the hand grenade he was carrying. If he was carrying a pistol, he would load and unload it in front of us. He did this all day long. The message was clear: 'If you try to do anything, I'll happily kill you.'

There had been several rounds of talks between the negotiators and the hijackers, another round would begin in a few hours, late in the evening. The passengers, for all the optimism, remained in the aircraft. The hijackers were still at their bloody-minded best: they wanted all the militants on their list freed, and the sooner the better. But the days of grinding negotiations had made a dent. They finally dropped their demand for US $200 million and for the body of Sajjad Afghani. But they refused to retract on Maulana and the other thirty-five terrorists.

The negotiators were trying. They offered the hijackers another plane and crew instead of the battered A300 and Captain Sharan's weary crew. The offer was curtly refused. The hijackers were suspicious that there would be commandos hiding inside the new plane. The negotiators tried again, with each successive round trying to take more time and wear the hijackers out. Every day, psychologists said, meant more pressure on them. The stress could break them, but there was also the danger that they could go berserk and shoot the passengers.

The thirty-six militants were in different jails. They had to be tracked down. This would take a lot of time, especially tying up the legal loose ends. Also, many of them, including the Maulana, were in jails in Jammu and Kashmir. It would be difficult to persuade the chief minister, Farooq Abdullah, to agree to release them. The hijackers weren't swayed by these arguments. They wanted the militants released. Otherwise, they threatened to blow up the plane along with the passengers.

Whose side was the Taliban on? The hijackers did not seem to be worried at all about making a getaway. Yet, the Taliban had made the hijackers moderate certain demands, such as dropping the demand for money, as they were un-Islamic, Taliban Foreign Minister Muttawakil said. The Taliban seemed anxious to disassociate themselves from the problem. 'If the Indian side doesn't peacefully solve the problem, our next step will be to ask the hijackers to leave immediately. Otherwise, we will force them to leave,' Muttawakil said. Were there fears in the Taliban that India was readying for an Entebbe-style rescue operation? No one was sure. But Muttawakil wouldn't specify how long the Taliban were willing to accommodate the hijackers. 'We are not here to set deadlines. We are here to find a peaceful solution.'

Despite all the tension in the plane and in the terminal building where the negotiators were, only the occasional noise of the Airbus engines broke the stillness of the Kandahar day. A bearded Taliban guard in a shawl cycled past the plane. Others sat in the sunshine, playing with their assault rifles. In a distance were parked old Russian helicopters and planes, which probably were not in any state to be ever used again. Within the terminal, however, there was the frantic activity of the UN and other officials. The discussions between the negotiators and the hijackers continued interminably.

India was in a position where it was forced to praise the Taliban, whose government it didn't recognize, for helping out in a time of crisis. The only other way of reaching out to the Taliban was through two of the three countries that recognized them—Saudi Arabia and the UAE. Pakistan, the third, was understandably a different issue.

In New Delhi, the parliamentary affairs minister, Pramod Mahajan said, 'The government has responded appropriately,' whatever that meant. He assured reporters the passengers were safe, though not in good shape. Consultations with the armed forces continued. For the second day, the three chiefs met the cabinet committee on security. But it was accepted that there could be little military involvement, except perhaps intelligence inputs, unless the Taliban government agreed, which seemed unlikely.

Far away in Chennai, L.K. Advani, like Jaswant Singh, had praise for the Taliban. At the BJP's national council, he said India was 'greatly encouraged' by the Taliban's warning to the hijackers that if they tried to shoot passengers, the Taliban militia would storm the plane.

The government's only achievement was a public relation one: the mood of the relatives of the passengers was now less hostile. After their earlier outbursts, most could now only wait and hope, and request the government not to give into unreasonable demands. But many weren't complimentary of the government's briefings.

'They always give us stale news anyway. We come here only to interact with other relatives,' said Dr Kailash Singhal. His brother-in-law and his wife were on the hijacked plane. Many of the relatives had come to New Delhi from Haldwani, Kolkata, Vellore, and other places. They kept in touch with one another. Whenever someone had new information, it would be quickly passed on. A tragedy had brought strangers close. There was no slogan-shouting or loud criticism, only hope and prayer. At a gurudwara in Punjabi Bagh, the relatives of passengers and crew attended a prayer meeting. Navneet Sharan recited a hymn. It was the best relatives could do.

Chapter Ten

Kandahar

30 December 1999

I must have been asleep for a couple of hours. At about 2 a.m., there was a shout and then there was confusion everywhere. 'All of you, get back to your seats immediately,' Burger shouted. Those passengers sleeping in the executive class stumbled back to the economy class in the darkness, dazed and half-asleep.

'What's going on?' I asked him.

'Nothing at all. You go back to sleep.' Then he turned to shout at the more slow-moving passengers. 'Get out, get out. And quickly. Otherwise, I'll shoot.'

Within minutes, the executive class was virtually empty. Only a few of the more ill passengers who could not move were left. I was too tired to stay awake and dropped off soon after.

I woke up again at 5 a.m. when Doctor came to summon Mr Jaggia. I was still half-awake when he returned from his meeting with Chief.

'What did he say?' I asked as usual.

'The talks have failed. We are back to square one.'

'Why did they break down?' I was really alarmed.

Mr Jaggia said Chief was very edgy. The Taliban soldiers were outside. They had lit a bonfire near a plane because it was very cold. Their presence was making him nervous.

Chief had said that the plane should be refueled. 'We have to move from here,' he had said.

'Why do you need to do that?' Mr Jaggia had asked.

'There is no point in even talking with your government. We have nothing to say to your officials.'

'Why don't you try just one more time?' Mr Jaggia had requested.

'No.'

'The plane needs maintenance before it can fly again!'

'Why don't you do it yourself? You're a senior man. You're about to retire. You probably know enough about the plane. So do what you must do and let's get out of here.'

When Mr Jaggia was still unwilling, Chief had said, 'I'll talk to your commander.' He probably thought he could persuade me. Chief had then made a startling statement, Mr Jaggia told me. He wanted the plane to be flown back to Amritsar! He felt that a breakthrough could be arrived at in Amritsar.

The flight engineer was very afraid. He thought they would blow up the plane after take-off. Chief wanted enough fuel for five hours. He said he wanted to fly all around the world. He felt there would be a decision somewhere. In weariness and frustration, he seemed to be saying different things at different times.

Listening to Mr Jaggia, I was afraid that this was the end. The talks had broken down, the hijackers were on the warpath and there was nothing we could do. But still hope lurked somewhere; I felt I wasn't meant to die like this. I sat brooding in my seat. Burger came out of the cockpit and asked Mr Jaggia to move to the rear of the cabin. I think they didn't want me to know about his discussions with Chief. But he had already told me.

An hour later, Burger returned in a foul mood.

'All of you... You've slept enough. Now get up. We have been very nice to you all this while. We have decided to behave the way hijackers do.'

I thought our time had finally come. With the failure of the negotiations, the hijackers were now set on destruction. I had to do something. We just couldn't be killed one by one.

'I want to speak to Chief,' I said desperately.

'You sit quietly,' he said.

I tried again. 'Just give me one last chance. I have to speak to your Chief.'

'No. No discussions will be held.'

'Okay, just do this. Please ask him if he will speak to me for a moment. That's all I am asking.'

Burger left reluctantly and was soon back. Chief had agreed to speak to me. I felt he was the least hotheaded, maybe I could persuade him not to harm the passengers.

'What is the problem?' I asked him as I went into the cockpit.

'There will be no more discussions, no more time-wasting talk,' he said.

'Please let me do something. I can speak with the negotiators directly if you wish,' I answered.

'You won't speak, and I won't speak. Those negotiators are sons of bitches. There is no point in speaking with them. So far,

I have been listening to the negotiators. Now we will do what I want done.'

I glanced outside. The tarmac was full of Taliban commandos. They were standing close to the plane, ten feet from each other. It was a reassuring sign. They must have closed in after the talks had failed. It meant that something could still happen. The Taliban were not abandoning us completely. The hijackers could still be persuaded to release the passengers. Or the plane would be stormed. It meant at least that if the hijackers began to kill people, the Taliban would take action.

At that moment, I longed for something decisive to happen. We couldn't stay on the plane indefinitely for much longer. Something had to happen. If the commandos began their operation, we could also take supporting action inside the plane.

I tried persuasion again. 'Chief sahab, let me speak to them,' I said. I touched his feet twice. 'Maybe I'll be able to make them understand your point.'

He refused. 'I won't speak to them, and I won't let you speak to them. If I do, they'll think I am weak. Now we'll do what we want to.'

He sent me back to my seat. 'lt wasn't going to be a good morning,' I thought.

The plane was a sorry sight. The toilets were overflowing and evidence of the chaos of the last six days was everywhere. I was beginning to forget what a proud plane it once was. The passengers looked heart-wrenchingly weary and despondent.

Shortly afterwards, the hijackers started waking up the people who had dozed off. 'Get up, get up,' they said.

They hadn't done anything like this before. Now I was really afraid.

Burger started to speak. He said the Indian government really did not want us freed and that the negotiators thought all this was a joke. 'Now,' he said, 'it is time to show the Indian government we mean business. We will kill the hostages, one by one. Don't believe that when the first man is shot, the others will survive. When we start shooting, everyone will die.'

I had lived in fear since Christmas Eve, but I had never been so afraid before. Everything was finally over.

They opened the doors of the aircraft, ostensibly for fresh air, but I later realized it was probably superstition. They wanted the souls of the people they killed to have space to leave. Whatever the reason, the fresh air was a relief. The stench from the toilets had filled the plane, and the air was very stale. We were all feeling very nauseous that morning. Now, we began to freeze. The auxiliary power unit had broken down again and the bitterly cold Kandahar morning air rushed in through the open doors. Everyone was shivering; it was both fear and the cold.

I looked at the crew and the passengers and wondered whom they would kill first. What were all of them thinking? Did they realize that this was the end?

There was still our hurriedly planned retaliatory move. I had briefed a few passengers and the crew about this. It was always meant to be the last resort, when all hope was gone. If they started killing people, we would attack them and try to overpower them. Desperate situations call for desperate measures. One or two or perhaps even twenty of us would die, but at least over a hundred of us would be saved. If we let them shoot us, one by one, they would all live and none of us would. Now that the talks had broken down and the killings seemed about to begin, this was all we could do.

I thought they would perhaps first kill passengers who were travelling alone. Then they would start on the others. I wondered when they would start shooting. When the time came, we had planned that I would shout 'Evacuate', and we would all fall on the hijackers, and run, fight and save ourselves. Burger returned to the cabin once more. '*Aap apne apne bhagwan ko yaad kar lijiye* (All of you, say your last prayers),' he said.

I knew they were serious. Each passenger put his or her head down. No one said a word. I saw the faces, tight with tension. They had hoped and prayed for release and now it was all over. The days of agonized waiting had come to this.

'Now you join me in a prayer. It will do you some good,' he announced.

To me, it seemed as if this was being done on purpose. It is easier to kill people when they are praying rather than when they are coming at you.

Burger began by invoking Allah. The prayer was filled with Urdu words which he murmured to himself. I could not follow what he was saying. He walked down the aisle and reached the central galley. I decided I had to speak to him. Maybe there was a way out, maybe I could still persuade him. Of all the hijackers, he was the most friendly and approachable. I was hoping desperately he would listen to me. I got up and followed him to the galley.

'Mr Burger, are you seriously thinking of killing people? If yes, will you do me a favor?'

'Yes, what?'

'Will you kill me first? I am the commander of the plane. I would like to die first.' I thought that at least some of the passengers could escape in the confusion.

Burger was silent for a moment.

'*Aisa hain, Captain sahab.* (It's like this, Captain sahab.) You're not going to die. And nor will I. There will be some solution.'

'If that is what you think, why don't you allow me to speak to the negotiators?'

'We cannot sit and talk with those people. They are useless. We are still looking for a solution and we feel there will be one.'

'If that is so, why are you troubling the passengers? They are so tense.'

'We must do it. The situation is such.'

We continued to talk for ten minutes in the cramped galley. The gloom was lifting, the tension gradually ebbing. We were not going to die right now.

'You believe in God. And I believe in God. We will have a solution, and my passengers and crew will be safe,' I told him. I hugged him and went back to my seat.

It was a morning not one of us will ever forget.

'It keeps coming back, the jitters that began on 30 December,' said passenger Ramesh Grover. 'The hijackers had asked us to say our last prayers. The negotiations had failed, and I think they were contemplating two things that morning: either taking off and blowing the plane up in mid-air or shooting the passengers one by one. I remember the silence in the aircraft though one or two people got hysterical.' Grover realized that they had reached a point of no return. They were going to shoot him. 'Do what you want to do. Let's get over with it. Enough is enough,' he told the hijackers in his mind.

Grover remembers the fanaticism of the hijackers. 'They would not have hesitated to die for their cause. If Chief had said "You have to die," they would have willingly died.' Bhola, he remembers was 'the littlest of them but enough of a terror.' And Shankar was very intimidating too. 'You should have seen his eyes, like the colored marbles we played with as children. They protruded, like a toad's eyes.'

A little later, Burger called for Kobita Mukherjee. 'Make some tea for the hijackers and crew,' he told her.

When Kobita returned ten minutes later, the tray in her hand, I was amazed. 'Things are so tense, and you went off to make tea!'

'Burger told me to,' she answered.

If Burger wanted us to drink tea, he wasn't going to kill us, at least not immediately. The tension ebbed further. We would live longer than I thought.

I went up to Burger. 'What are you planning?'

'Drink your tea and then I'll tell you.'

About ten minutes later, he came to talk to me. 'The Taliban government's foreign ministry officials have intervened. They have told us to start talks again. We had broken off but as we have a lot of respect for the minister, we are going to start negotiations again.'

'I want to tell my passengers this,' I said.

He went to ask Chief for permission and came back.

'Yes, you can tell your passengers.'

I picked up the red megaphone they used. 'I have some news for you,' I began. 'I would like to tell you that negotiations have begun again at the request of the foreign minister of Afghanistan. I would request you to pray to God to ensure the talks are successful so that we can go home safely.'

I sat in my seat, shut my eyes and began praying. I hadn't prayed with such devotion and intensity since the hijacking began, but it seemed appropriate now. I didn't believe in God too much, and besides I had always saved prayer as the last resort. There's no point calling God all the time, human beings should be capable of taking care of themselves. But I called Him now. All of us needed His intervention at some points in our lives. I had never felt so helpless.

I must have sat like that for five minutes and prayed with great intensity. 'God, you know how patient all of us have been over these last five to six days. Please save these innocent people. They haven't done anything wrong.'

I don't believe in miracles, but I think my prayers were answered.

Shortly afterwards, around three in the afternoon, Burger came over. 'The talks are through. There has been a breakthrough,' he said.

'What happened?' I asked.

'They have agreed to release three of our people.'

They shut the plane doors once more and the stench was with us again. But I didn't care. The news was too overwhelming. Burger picked up the megaphone. He told people that the talks were over. 'Now, you will be released.' I could see the faces of the passengers. There was bewilderment and disbelief. We had teetered between life and death for so many days. Death had been so close that morning that this last-minute reprieve wasn't something we would accept as final. We were still on the plane, guarded by armed hijackers in Kandahar. We weren't home yet.

A low buzz of conversation broke out. 'Why have they closed the doors? If a decision has been taken, they should let us all go,' one passenger asked.

As people talked, some gradually came round to the idea of being freed. I noticed that one or two passengers were looking at me. 'What do you think? Is this the truth?' one said.

I turned to Burger. 'Can I meet Chief?'

'Yes,' he agreed. I went inside.

'Can you tell me what has happened?'

'Three of our friends have been released,' Chief replied. He said the 'exchange' would take eight to ten hours.

After the Indian government released his three friends, he would let the passengers and the crew go.

'Is this the truth? Or is it just another promise?' I asked.

'Don't worry at all. This is a guarantee.'

I wanted to speak to the negotiators. When he agreed, I called the ATC on the walkie-talkie. 'What is the truth?' I asked, when one of the negotiators came online.

'The decision has been taken. Tell your passengers. They shouldn't worry any more. The exchange will take place either tonight or tomorrow morning.'

Before walking out, I shook hands with Chief. 'I am grateful to God that the passengers and the crew have been saved. Beyond that, I don't have anything to say,' I told him.

In the cabin, Doctor was speaking to the passengers, using the red megaphone. He had been speaking about the greatness of Islam in Urdu for a while. 'God has given you a mind. All of you should embrace Islam. Then you will be able to experience the wonders of the religion. It is the best religion in the world. Read the Koran.' After that, Doctor spoke about the situation in Chechnya. He was all praise for the 'freedom-fighters'. 'They are fighting for their cause, and they are fighting for Islam,' he said. Then he started to extol the virtues of the dreaded Osama bin Laden.

Bhola, standing nearby, also joined the paean. 'Do you know about him? The Saudi Arabians threw him out. He has been given shelter here. He is a wealthy man. Also, a very nice man. He can buy up the US and he can buy up India most certainly. And despite his wealth, he lives in the jungles here. All for Islam. He has great regard for Islam and he is fighting for the cause, for Muslims all over the world,' he said. Doctor continued. 'When you get home, read the Koran. You will learn about the greatness of Islam.'

Such sermonizing, Romesh Grover felt 'was part of what the hijackers saw as their job. But it was an absolute failure. Even the circumstances were not conducive to such sermonizing.'

During these lessons, the passengers pretended to listen with rapt attention, and they clapped at the end.

After Doctor and Bhola finished speaking, the passengers swarmed towards me. 'Tell us about what is happening,' they said.

I picked up the megaphone. I told the passengers that I had talked to the negotiators, and they had confirmed what Burger had said. We would be freed either later this evening or some time tomorrow. I thanked them for their exemplary courage and fortitude.

By early afternoon, the news had sunk in, and the clouds had lifted. I could see the first wary smiles, the enthusiastic chatter and even some laughter. No one even complained about the stench from the toilets and the lack of breakfast. They were too busy playing bridge and bluff. Even the hijackers seemed happier. Though they still carried their weapons, they seemed a lot less wary.

There was a pervading sensation of strangeness. 'There was a sense of relief. Yet I couldn't completely believe they would let us go. I didn't believe it would happen. After being with them for five or six days, I had reservations about them. Those last twenty-six hours were difficult,' said Grover.

Lunch arrived, but the passengers didn't seem to care. But there was enthusiasm about the chilled cans of Pepsi that came with lunch. There was only half a can per passenger as there weren't enough supplies in Kandahar. I wondered how the Taliban allowed a product manufactured by the US in their country. Then I looked at the cans. They were imported from Pakistan. The lunch had also come from Islamabad, the UN apparently supplied it. There were burgers and sweets. Some were too excited to eat, and others remembered the state of the toilets. But some just ate and ate; it was perhaps the ebbing away of tension. The cabin crew hadn't had much to eat over the last six days, and today, Burger sauntered over. 'I am like your elder brother. Please eat something today,' he said to one of the air hostesses.

He wandered over to another of the air hostesses, whom he called didi. 'What kind of an education have you had?' he asked.

She said she had an undergraduate degree. 'What about you?' she asked.

'I am an MBBF,' he joked. 'A matric bar failed.'

He asked some of the crew about their families and then went to speak to the passengers. Many of them wrote down their addresses for him. Burger even wrote down a contact address for himself! I wonder why he did that. Maybe it would be a way of tracking him and all the others now. There were people whose boarding cards he autographed. I was afraid the passengers would pass on their real addresses; they were hijackers after all. When Burger wrote anything down, I rejoiced. I was sure a handwriting sample would help investigators later.

The toilets in the back were a lost cause by then. In the evening, we requested the hijackers for permission to use the toilets in the front, the ones they were using. They were also in bad condition, but better than the other ones.

As the end now seemed in sight, the hijackers made what appeared to be a concession. All these days the passengers were forced to sit in places decided upon by the hijackers. They had moved everyone to the back of the cabin. Now they wanted the passengers to go back to their original seats and sit with their friends and family. The passengers refused.

'We spent the bad days sitting next to people we didn't know at all. We want to share the few good hours with them as well,' one of them said.

All the passengers who were ill revived miraculously at the news of imminent freedom. It made me happy to see their laughing faces. I did wonder what lay behind this though. Were they ill to begin with? Were small illnesses aggravated by the stress? Or were some of them trying to pull off hoaxes in order to get off the plane?

There had been such a dramatic change that day that I think we were exhausted by having run through a whole range of emotions from intense despair at the certainty of death to the long-awaited news of approaching freedom. I thought of those moments now when we were asked to say our last prayers, the hijackers running around the cabin, Burger screaming at us, and more chillingly, telling the other hijackers, 'Pull out the pins from the grenades and leave them next to the door. Roll a few under the chairs.' We were afraid to move. They threatened to blow up the plane if anyone blinked. I was sitting next to Rajni during those terrible moments. She was the bravest of the lot and she was crying, afraid that she would die in one apocalyptic moment when the hijackers blew up the plane. She had been a great help during the darkest hours and the sight of her crying had upset me. If Rajni has lost hope, the others must be feeling terrible, I had thought. 'Please don't break down. This is a time to remain strong. This is our biggest test,' I had told her. Throughout the agony that began on Christmas Eve, we had hoped, even when there was no hope. Whenever the thought of death occurred to me, I tried to push it out of my mind. Whenever you think about dying, you die. Late that afternoon, the realization that we would be free, sooner or later, came to me. My knees were wobbly as I sat down. I offered a silent prayer of thanks.

There was another scary moment that day. Chief summoned Mr Jaggia to the cockpit. He had one last kamikaze wish. 'Please refuel the plane and fly back to Amritsar if you wish. On the way, plan a detour and fly over the sea. We jump off!' he told Mr Jaggia, in all seriousness perhaps. Mr Jaggia evaded the issue.

The hijackers seemed so focused most of the time, and then Chief would suddenly have one of these bizarre ideas.

In the evening, everyone looked cheerful. It was a 'we-have-to-get-home' feeling. People were talking about who would receive them at the airport, and what sleeping on a bed would feel like after a week on a cold A300 seat.

When dinner arrived, it was the usual fare, and a lot of oranges and apples. It was finally the last supper on the plane, but people ate very little; I don't know whether it was the excitement or the terror of going to the toilet.

Many passengers remembered the toilets with a shudder.

'They were so bad, I didn't go near one for five days,' said R.K. Ghosh. Ramesh Grover declared, 'After seeing toilets like that, you can stop going to them altogether! They were so bad.'

Others spoke of fear. Jeanne Moore, the American, was asked about coffins during the negotiations when the hijackers wanted Sajjad Afghani's body returned. 'When they approached me and asked what you call the box to keep a body, I thought it was for me,' she remembered. She wrote the word coffin on a piece of paper and gave it to the hijackers.

Late that night, there was another crisis, unexpected and unforeseen. A young boy, barely ten and travelling with his father, fell ill. Why he hadn't got off the plane in Dubai isn't clear, but he had high temperature, he was shivering. 'We made him lie down,' Kar said, 'and I walked up to Burger. "*Ladke ko itna bukhar hain. Mujhe barf chahiye*. (The boy has high fever. I need ice.)" I said. The hijacker knew the deal was done, that it would all come to an end in a few hours, and didn't want anything to go wrong. They'd killed Katyal; they were afraid a mishap would create additional problems. They found ice, they found paracetamol tablets and gradually, the fever came down. They were tense. All of them, Burger, Shankar, Doctor and Bhola were running around. They knew the deal was done, they knew Maulana Masood Azhar and the other two were coming. They didn't want anything to happen to the boy," Kar said.

That evening, Kar spoke with Burger. '*Aap Islam ko kyun mante hain*? (Why are you a Muslim?) There are other religions in the world,' Kar asked. 'Why don't you respect them?' That's when Burger replied: '*Hum rukenge nahin tab tak jab tak sari duniya ek takht and ek taaj ke niche na aa jaye*. (We will not wait till the world is under one form and one crown.)'

'That is something that remained with me, because what he said is so radical. And this is the same guy who had said: "Look, we are very ordinary people. We are very loving. We have not touched your women. We have done nothing wrong."'

All this while, I wondered what the night would be like. And for all the excitement, it was a disappointment. For there was no word of release: there was a delay at the other end and word did not filter through. Still, it didn't lower morale. 'Okay, we can't go today. We'll go tomorrow,' one passenger said. Till midnight, the passengers were full of jokes and chatter.

There was a Nepalese passenger, Mr Gajinder Singh, a well-known comic actor. He was a remarkable mimic. Gajinder did a great imitation of Gabbar Singh from *Sholay*. He also did a wonderful impersonation of Bhola. But Bhola wasn't amused. He stormed in and slapped Gajinder. We were very upset with Bhola, and I complained to Burger. 'There was no need for Bhola to be so aggressive,' I said.

Burger cautioned Bhola.

Before we packed in for the night, we had a visit from Burger. He wanted alms for the Afghans. 'Think about it. You were in Afghanistan for all these days. The people here gave you food and water. They ensured you were safe. Don't you think you should donate something for the poor?'

'There is a hospital for children here. Maybe you should collect money for it. Don't give me the money. One of you take responsibility for the cash.'

Four or five people immediately stood up. People were digging into their pockets, and I could see five-hundred-rupee notes coming out. The volunteers went from passenger to passenger with plastic bags and managed to collect about 71,000 rupees. It would go to the children of Afghanistan, they said.

Burger slipped into the cockpit for a while. He came back for an announcement. 'I hadn't asked Chief for permission before I suggested all of you contribute. I spoke with him just now and he has agreed.'

Saibal Kar and Sanjeev Sharma took on the responsibility of purchasing gifts for the Afghan children and leaving them with the Afghan Embassy in New Delhi. No one remembered at that point that it wasn't controlled by the Taliban.

Roberto was in such high spirits that he was joking about the money. As the volunteers walked around, plastic bag in hand, he chased them, shouting, 'You are my friends. I need the money.'

Christina, his girlfriend, and Mr Jaggia again spent time together that evening. They talked about Switzerland. She invited the crew there. 'We will leave our cars and private plane at your disposal. You can go wherever you want,' she said.

'Where are you planning to go now?' I asked her.

'To Goa,' she said. 'Why don't you tell Roberto that we should go to Goa? We shouldn't skip Goa, having come all the way. He wants to go back home after this ordeal.'

I did suggest going to Goa to him, but he said he was too exhausted. He couldn't take any more travelling for a while. I sympathized with that.

Late in the evening, I noticed several passengers looking very morose. I walked up to them. 'We'll be home in a few hours. Why are you looking troubled?'

'I am not happy with the Indian government's decision,' one passenger said. 'Why are they releasing terrorists?'

'Look, it's the government's decision. Storming the plane or releasing terrorists, it is the government's wish. There is nothing we can do. At least you're going home. You will be with your family. Think about it...you could have been killed if the commandos had stormed the plane! This is not the moment to be unhappy.'

'Yes,' he slowly nodded. 'You may be right.'

I didn't want to stay the night in Kandahar. I was so tired of the cold and the discomfort. I felt a little less burdened about the passengers. I was wondering how my wife and daughters were, and the longing to see them was intense.

Tomorrow, I said to myself, I will cease to be the commander of IC 814. I hope my wife is there to receive me at the airport. I was wondering what she would be wearing the pink salwar kameez with the matching pearls she had promised to wear when I was to meet her at Hyderabad to go to Sharjah together? Would she bring Deeksha and Aashna along? What would I say to them? There were tears in my eyes, and it took me a while to pull myself together. Home was so close that I couldn't bear to wait.

The negotiations really started moving after the Taliban began mediating. The hijackers dropped their 'unIslamic' demand for US $200 million and for the return of Sajjid Afghani's body. India wanted the passengers, the crew and the A300. Now it was a matter of merely coming to an agreement about the number of militants to be released. Not thirty-five surely, not even fifteen. It would have to be a face-saving number. Which militants? Would

India decide or the hijackers? And then there was the question of safe passage for the hijackers. Would India agree to that?

The Taliban foreign minister was the shuttle diplomat. No longer were there just two sides (the Indian negotiators and the hijackers), but the bearded and bespectacled Muttawakil was an integral part of the proceedings. In India, a morning cabinet meeting, chaired by the prime minister, had cleared the move, and allowed the negotiators to bargain about the number of hostages. The negotiations, said Jaswant Singh, early in the day, were 'extremely delicately poised'.

Erick de Mul, the original UN negotiator, was back in Kandahar, but largely out of the picture. Another UN official had met one of the hijackers. The hijacker 'was lucid, calm, collected and committed whatever he seemed to be prepared to achieve,' the official said.

Behind the wall of denials, the truth was trickling out. Muttawakil had earlier spoken of the bargaining. Initially, he had brought down the number of militants to be released to fifteen. But even fifteen for 160-odd wasn't a respectable enough equation. It would mean international criticism for bowing to the hijackers; it wouldn't be acceptable in India either. Vajpayee had spoken of not bowing to the hijackers on Christmas Day. Yet, before New Year's Eve, there was talk of surrender. India couldn't accept releasing fifteen hardcore militants. There were also different interpretations of Muttawakil's role. Was he playing honest broker or was he playing both sides for international recognition for his pariah government?

The Taliban had no sympathy for the hijackers, was his official position. What they had done was against Islam, he told the *New York Times* in a telephonic interview. He ascribed the Taliban's intervention to humanitarian concerns. Meanwhile, he would try to renegotiate with the hijackers. Fifteen were too many, he would tell them. They had to settle for five.

And after more talks, the hijackers and negotiators decided that Maulana Masood Azhar and two others would be released, and the hijackers would be allowed safe passage. It was a bitter pill for the Indians. The hijackers had killed Ripin Katyal and now they would escape justice. The deal was finally clinched though Doval would later say the negotiators wished they had a little more time. Another day or two, and it would have been better, much better for India. Unless the hijackers had a final rush of adrenalin and chose a fiery martyrdom by blowing up the plane along with their hostages, the passengers would be home for the New Year.

One passenger was already back via Islamabad: Anil Khurana, the diabetes patient, his blood-sugar levels alarmingly high, and suffering from a throat infection that prevented him from eating. He was feeling intensely guilty too at having left the others, including his brother-in-law Sanjeev Sharma, behind. He burst into tears when he saw his wife in Islamabad.

The Kandahar airport Khurana left behind looked different now. A tank, several armoured personnel carriers and multi-barreled rocket launchers were guarding the airport, a little too much to use against five hijackers carrying revolvers and grenades. That evening, Jaswant Singh had spoken of Taliban armed forces reinforcing the airport. But were the soldiers there as a warning to the hijackers? Or were they there to ensure there would be no commando operation against the plane? A rescue operation, senior armed forces officers said, would mean war. All the while, the NSG commandos were still in Kandahar, waiting in the A320 aircraft, waiting for the opportunity that would never come.

Chapter Eleven

Kandahar

31 December 1999

There were doubts about getting home yesterday. There were none about today. When I woke up at 7 a.m., I was relaxed. There was a sense of joy in my heart. Uncomfortable perhaps, and not as clean as I would have liked to have been, but happy. Tonight, I would be at home with my wife and children. I would have a decent meal (the brown rice with raisins was really getting to me) and a comfortable bed to sleep in. Best of all, I would savor the taste of freedom. I would know I had lived through hell.

Then I remembered that my work wasn't over. I wasn't sure how we would get home. Would I have to fly my passengers back to New Delhi on this aircraft? Or would I have to escort them back on another aircraft? Either way, I still had a responsibility to them.

Meanwhile, Chief summoned the flight engineer. He wanted Mr Jaggia to go down with Shankar to the hold and pull out a second bag.

'This is a dangerous bag,' Chief said. 'We don't want to cause you any trouble. We don't want to leave it behind.'

Mr Jaggia asked Chief to get him some help from the airport engineers. Getting to the hold would be difficult.

There had been no power in the plane all night and it was very cold. The hydraulic pumps that are needed to open the doors run on electricity.

There was an atmosphere of hope pervading the cabin. It was untidy and smelly as usual. But most people, including the doubters who still weren't sure whether we would get back, were much more relaxed. There was an antakshari game in progress. Others were chatting amongst themselves or humming. I even saw one or two people praying, perhaps in thanksgiving that they were going back alive. I spoke to every passenger that morning. I told them the same thing. 'We are going back. You have my guarantee.'

The doors were opened, and the chilly Kandahar air rushed in, but at least the stink went away after a while. There was breakfast: cold milk, biscuits, tea and fruits. With breakfast came an unexpected gift: toothpaste and some toothbrushes. We couldn't use the toilets anymore, so the galley became a temporary washroom. Many wanted to freshen up in order to look good when they reached Delhi. In these eight days, we had all become very scruffy looking. Now, normalcy was returning slowly. But not everyone wanted to clean up. I heard someone say, 'I haven't brushed my teeth for a week. Why should I brush today?' It was an argument I couldn't really understand.

After breakfast, there was a last burst of indoctrination. 'Doctor will lecture you about the tenets of Islam,' Burger solemnly announced.

'Islam is a great religion. Become a believer,' Doctor, who had killed Katyal, began. I don't remember all the things he said, but I remember some bits.

'When you go to the market to buy vegetables, you know what is good and what is not. You also know which religion is good and which is not. So, use your brains and choose your religion.' He again praised Osama bin Laden.

He went on to discuss the Jammu and Kashmir issue. He blamed the Indian army for the situation there.

But the passengers gradually got impatient. They had been on the plane for a week. And now they wanted to be released. They weren't keen on a lesson on Islam.

At lunchtime, Chief again wanted the flight engineer to open the hold. Mr Jaggia went down and tried, but without electricity and even with a pump, it wasn't possible to open the door more than halfway. Someone went inside but couldn't locate the bag.

I waited eagerly to hear an aircraft, our own aircraft. In the afternoon, I heard a Boeing 737. No sound had ever sounded sweeter. I heard myself telling people, 'A Boeing 737, belonging to Alliance Air, a subsidiary of Indian Airlines, has arrived, hopefully with the three people the hijackers wanted released. We may be free very soon.'

It was over, bar the last-minute chats. Chief called me inside the cockpit. 'Captain Sahab, I want to thank you.'

'Thank you for what, being hostages for a week? For troubling you?'

'No, no. Please don't take it amiss. This was our mission, and this had to be done. There was nothing else we could do. If we have made mistakes or if we have caused you sorrow or discomfort, please forgive me. Also, please apologize to the passengers on my behalf. You have been with us for over a week. I hope you will support us and our cause in the future.'

Captain Sharan believed it was going to be his last day in Kandahar from the moment he woke up, but the decision in New Delhi was finalized a little later. The news from Kandahar was positive: the hijackers were ready to release the passengers and crew, provided the three militants of their choice were freed. When Jaswant Singh and Brajesh Mishra met the prime minister, he agreed. During the morning's cabinet committee on security meeting, Jaswant Singh volunteered to receive the passengers in Kandahar.

'It was his decision,' said Mansingh. 'He wanted to go because he didn't want any last-minute hitch. In case a decision had to be taken in Afghanistan, he would be there to take it. It wouldn't have to be referred to Delhi. For there was a concern that the hijackers would make yet another demand. Or the Taliban would spring a surprise.' Not everyone was happy with the decision. 'Katju (in Kandahar for the last five days) didn't want Jaswant Singh to go,' said Mansingh. 'I told him going to Kandahar may not be such a good idea. What if someone took him hostage?'

So, it was a risk, but then, the cabinet had approved the decision.

The prime minister spoke to President K.R. Narayanan, and the release of the Maulana from Jammu's Kot Bhalwal Jail, Mushtaq Ahmed Zargar from Srinagar Central Jail, and Ahmed Omar Syed Sheikh from New Delhi's Tihar Jail was ordered. A special aircraft was sent to bring back the two militants from Jammu and Kashmir. They were escorted to Delhi by the RAW chief, A.S. Dulat.

The hijackers had chosen well. The thirty-one-year-old Maulana, chief ideologue and general secretary of the Harkat ul-Ansar, and editor of the *Sada-e-Mujaheed*, didn't have blood on his hands: he was a motivator who got others to do the killing but both Zargar and Omar were killers. Zargar (called Latrum), a Kashmiri, had joined the Jammu and Kashmir Liberation Front, and had gone to Pakistan after the controversial 1987 elections in Jammu and Kashmir. Many had lost faith in the system after the polls, widely believed to have been rigged. He led the Al Umer Mujahideen, a group responsible for the murder of several members of the security forces in Jammu and Kashmir and many abductions. He had killed one of his own assistants, apparently an informer, before being arrested in May 1992.

Omar, only twenty-six, a martial arts expert and holding a degree from the prestigious London School of Economics, is the son of a wealthy London-based man. A British national, he was trained in Afghanistan and Pakistan, including a stint at a camp where the SSG, the Pakistan army's commando unit, go through their paces. His specialty was kidnapping foreign tourists and exchanging them for Harkat fighters in jail. He had kidnapped four tourists, including three Englishmen, and kept them in captivity for over a month. Two policemen, Inspector Dhruv Lal Yadav and Constable Ram Sevak, were killed in the operation to rescue them. One militant also died, and Omar and another militant, Abdul Rahim, were eventually arrested. Releasing him was a severe blow to the government.

All three militants were brought to Indira Gandhi International Airport's Technical Area with the foreign minister and security personnel. Omar was the first to arrive and was served breakfast at the airport. Many Tihar officials didn't know he had been released. The RAW plane from Jammu was delayed by fog and eventually arrived at 1 p.m. Security men with Maulana at the airport said he was in high spirits. 'He was behaving like a king after a long and hard battle. He was trying to joke with us,' one security man said. He could also rubbish the Indian government freely. No one was willing to risk a reply till the passengers and crew were freed. He ordered a police officer to remove his handcuffs and those of the other militants. In the special aircraft, they greeted each other warmly, saying it was an Id gift from their brother-militants. 'They have done what they promised,' they said to each other.

In the aircraft just before it took off, Mansingh spotted a well-known TV reporter. 'Who authorized you?' he asked her. 'She said she had authorization,' said Mansingh. 'I called Jaswant Singh and said: "I cannot send her." I asked him if I could throw her out. He agreed, and I said "Stay outside" to her.'

The plane carrying the external affairs minister and the terrorists left late, at 3 p.m. Immediately after that, Brajesh Mishra, the prime minister's principal secretary, at a press conference, defended the deal. Comparisons with the Rubaiya Sayeed episode were of course inevitable. 'This was the best deal... we are paying the price of terrorism. If seven militants could be released for one Rubaiya, what's wrong in releasing three for 170?' he said. The other option was to collect 170 bodies and the aircraft wreckage. There was also much rhetoric about India not being a soft state. 'We have to establish that we are not a soft state. It must be remembered the hijacking did not take place from any of the Indian airports.'

Later that evening, in his speech to the nation, the prime minister said he would continue to fight terrorism. 'India shall not spare any effort to thwart the phenomenon of terrorism itself... For two decades now, this menace has exacted a cruel price from us in India. Thousands of innocents, men, women and children have been done to death. Tens and thousands of families have lost their home and hearth,' he said. He had refused to bow to the hijackers on Christmas Eve. A week later, he now spoke about 'substantially scaling down their demands'. He called the hijacking 'evil and diabolic' and called upon all nations to unite and defeat terrorism.

At the evening's cabinet meeting, the home minister, L.K. Advani, expressed his unhappiness with the decision. A few more days of negotiation would have worn the hijackers down and secured the hostages' release without setting free three terrorists, he believed. He wondered whether he should resign.

It was 4.40 p.m. in Kandahar when Jaswant Singh stepped off the plane with the three militants. It would be a disappointing trip. He wanted to bring the hijackers to India, but the Taliban wouldn't agree. Muttawakil, the Taliban foreign minister, rejected this suggestion outright. The Taliban would only abide by the deal: the hijackers would be allowed safe passage. Moreover, the Taliban would also extract a huge bill for services rendered. These included the parking fee at Kandahar for the planes as well as other charges, including for the naans, the brown rice with raisins and everything else. Jaswant Singh did take some money with him, said Mansingh. 'It was a bill for the food and services that was provided to the passengers. It came to US $25,000. It was to an Islamabad account.' It was time to go home. The public cordiality with the Taliban continued. After returning to New Delhi that evening, Jaswant Singh underlined this: 'We have conveyed our gratitude to the Taliban and authorities in Afghanistan for the cooperation.' A grateful India's relationship with the Taliban hadn't changed, he added. The criticism was reserved for later. The well-armed Taliban militia could have easily overpowered the hijackers at Kandahar. Then they could have been tried under any law, even Taliban law, and the three militants would not have been released. But the Taliban refused.

As the hours passed, both the hostages and the hijackers became increasingly restive. Then Burger returned with news. 'Our three brothers, freedom-fighters are back. Now, please rearrange your seating positions,' he said. On the Boeing 737 that would take us back, he wanted the ill passengers in the front rows, followed by the women, and then the men. The air hostesses would sit behind the male passengers and bringing up the rear would be us—the co-pilot, the flight engineer, the flight pursers and I. Why did he do it? Simple, he wanted the patients and the women to get off the plane first when it landed in New Delhi. I, of course, would be the last off the plane.

'Please pick up your hand luggage from the executive class. Don't take anyone else's and keep your bags with yourself,' he advised, sounding like a schoolteacher. He also demanded that all women should cover their heads when they moved to the 737. The Taliban government, he said, did not appreciate women with uncovered heads. Also, no one was still allowed to look out of the windows. I was the only person who was permitted to look out of the windows and to roam around. I saw a lot of security personnel moving around on the tarmac. I think they feared a last minute commando raid as they were getting out, and they took precautions.

Burger made a last threat, couched in diplomatic language. 'I will keep a watch on newspaper articles and television programs on the hijacking. I will read what you have to say about us. I hope you say we treated you well. If I read that you were abused or manhandled, we will not forgive or forget. We will be back, to take revenge.'

He was more apprehensive about women talking about being molested. 'I want you to remember something. We don't touch women during Ramadan. So don't make up stories.' For Rajni, he had a compliment: 'You won't do anything like that; you are a strong woman.' During those last moments on the plane, Kar looking back, spotted Burger. 'I saw him limbering up. He was standing up and then, in one fluid motion, kicked one of the luggage racks! I realized how incredibly fit he was, how well trained he was. He was a commando.'

At the same time, Shankar talked to Rajinder. 'I want you to have this,' he said, pointing to his jacket, a rather impressive Adidas creation. Rajinder immediately refused.

It was also a time for belated apologies. Burger sought me out and hugged me. 'I have troubled you very much. Please apologize to the passengers on my behalf,' he said.

Doctor was also hovering around. '*Humare taraf se bahut sorry*. (My apologies for everything.)' He said he had no intention of killing Ripin Katyal, but it had happened by accident. 'Yes,' he admitted, 'I was responsible for the lapse.'

Great, I thought. He is pleading guilty to manslaughter and not murder. Say that to Mrs Katyal.

There was more evidence of the growing bonds between the hijackers and their hostages. 'We all love you. We all love you,' one of the passengers loudly proclaimed.

I had a last meeting with Chief. Burger and Doctor were in attendance. '*Captain sahab, kaam ho gaya hain aur hum jaa rahe hain*. (We've finished our work and we are leaving.) We couldn't recover the bag we were looking for in the hold. It is a dangerous bag. There are explosives inside the bag. It was the millennium gift I had in mind for the Indian government. I don't want any of you to be in danger,' he said. 'I have one request. As soon as you leave, please make sure you get your passengers out very quickly. And immediately. If it explodes, all of you will be in trouble.'

All this while, Shankar was rummaging in the cabin. He didn't seem to be able to find whatever he was looking for. Burger came and asked me. 'We're looking for our binoculars. Have you seen it?' He was desperate.

I realized it was the night-vision binoculars. They had unloaded some five backpacks in the cockpit.

A cream-colored van had driven up and was waiting for them next to the plane. Its windowpanes were tinted black.

Burger had time for a last goodbye. 'Inshallah, we will meet some day.'

When everyone laughed, he said, 'No, we will not meet.'

Even the Chief had a last-minute goodbye message for the passengers. He entered the cabin and said: 'Thank you, and sorry for the trouble.'

They left the plane with their hoods still on, through the cockpit main bay door. They were carrying their guns in case there was a last-minute shootout on the tarmac. Shankar got off first, then Burger, then Chief, followed by Doctor, and finally Bhola. All of them got into the van. The three terrorists were already sitting in the van. I later heard they drove off taking with them a Taliban official as hostage. According to the terms agreed upon, they had ten hours to leave Afghanistan.

As soon as they left, I took over. I picked up the megaphone. 'This hijacking was not your fault or our fault. It was fate, but I must thank you all for your cooperation and help. I am also grateful to my cabin crew, my flight engineer and my co-pilot who cooperated with me.'

I still had one last fear. Could they have left a ticking time bomb in our hand luggage? I asked everyone to check their hand luggage thoroughly for anything suspicious.

My announcement left the passengers in a tizzy. A frenzied check of the cabin luggage began and fortunately, nothing was found. I checked the cockpit to see there was nothing in our briefcases, no hand grenade nestling amidst our flight papers. Again, nothing was found.

I opened the door of the aircraft: there was no ladder. I could see Captain J.R.D. Rao and Captain Suri who had come with the relief crew. And of course, the negotiators, mostly IFS and IPS officers, and a host of Taliban security men. It was so ironic that we were finally free, but we could not leave the plane because of mechanical impediments.

I asked for the ladder. While I was waiting, we had the first guest on the plane since the hijacking: Captain Suri. He came up the way the hijackers had left, through the cockpit main bay door. The passengers were cheering as he walked in.

A ladder finally arrived. One of the negotiators followed; he congratulated us for our patience and fortitude. Again, there was talk of explosives in the hold. He assured us we would be home soon.

Meanwhile, the passengers were cheering, hugging and congratulating each other. The video cameras were out, and one would think a festival of sorts had begun. Some came over and hugged and kissed me.

Captain Suri came up with an Iridium satellite phone, hardly much bigger than a cordless phone. 'God has kept my promise to bhabhi. Better call home,' he said.

There were tears in my eyes as I shakily punched the numbers. By the time I was punching 1, 1, 5 and 2, the last four digits, I was crying. The phone was ringing in the house, the familiar comfortable ring I knew so well. It was Amrinder Singh, my brother-in-law, who picked up the phone.

'I can't believe it is you,' he said.

'We're free,' I said. 'We'll be back in the evening,' I told him.

My wife came on the line. 'Navneet, I am coming back, I am coming back,' was all I could say. My voice was so choked that I didn't know whether she could understand what I was saying.

There were many tears of joy. Mr Jaggia, Rajinder and the others called home too. When everyone had called, I picked up the phone again. I wanted to speak to my wife. Again, Amrinder picked up the phone. 'I want to speak with my wife. I am free again,' I said. I was crying uncontrollably. They were tears of joy. This time I managed to say hello to my daughters as well.

I shook hands ceremoniously with Mr Jaggia and Rajinder. It was a big moment for all of us. It felt as if we had been reborn.

The ladder for the passengers was finally hooked onto the plane. I had one last task. During the excited moments of celebration that had been taking place, I had been scared that someone might get too excited and fall off the plane out of the open doorway. So, I had been guarding the door.

Now I was the first person to step onto the ladder, to check it was properly secured. But I didn't want to leave right then, I wanted each passenger to leave before me.

'Let this end the way a normal flight does. One of you stand at the door with folded hands. The others help the passengers get down. Remember, all's well that ends well,' I told the cabin crew.

The passengers left the plane in the sequence Burger had ordered. First the passengers who were ill, followed by the women, their heads covered with their dupattas or pallus. The foreign women used handkerchiefs. I stood to the left of the door, and as the passengers got down, laughing and joking, some of them shook hands with me. Halfway down the ladder stood Captain J.R.D. Rao. He too helped the passengers down. Two security personnel of the Taliban government also hovered around.

After the women had all left, the men came down. Some hugged me before they walked down. Many thanked the crew and me for our help. Then the plane was virtually empty. Only the crew were left.

'Take your baggage and walk down,' I said.

'After you, sir,' they said. Rajni was insistent that she would get off last, but I overruled her.

'No, I'll get off last.'

The cabin crew got off. There was only Mr Jaggia, Rajinder and me. Mr Jaggia and I embraced.

'I must thank you for your cooperation and for your good advice during these difficult times. I am thankful to you. Your experience was a great help.'

He took his bag and got off.

I turned to Rajinder, unassuming but always efficient. I hugged him. 'Captain Kumar, I'll remember your cooperation.'

'It was a team effort,' he said. 'That's why we managed to save the maximum number of passengers.' Then he left.

Standing in the cockpit, I looked around, panels of switches in front, on my right and behind me. My eyes travelled all over the little cockpit, the blue sun visor, the red fire handle, a green sun visor in front, the four seats with their turquoise blue and green covers, including the extra one on the left, and the rubberized carpeting. They lingered on each of the things I had worked with: the airspeed indicator, the control column, the white nose-wheel tiller on the left for ground steering with the color peeling off slightly, the throttle on the right for power. The cockpit was a squalid mess; it was littered with empty soda cans, papers and other rubbish. It didn't look like a cockpit at all.

I seemed to be the only one left. A thought struck me. No one should be left behind.

I ran back and looked around, behind the seats, in the galleys, everywhere. I also looked for a large package—in case there was a bomb. I checked the toilets. I didn't want anyone left there unconscious. I checked the executive class and the economy class. Reassured that no one was left. I returned to the cockpit. I picked up my black flight bag.

Another look around and I spotted something. It was the night-vision binoculars the hijackers used. I put it in my flight bag before I walked out. It was a happy moment, a moment of great relief. I could only say a silent prayer of thanksgiving that it had ended with minimal loss of life.

I felt terrible about Ripin Katyal. Though that was hardly in my hands, I still felt somehow responsible.

As I got down, Captain J.R.D. Rao hugged me. 'Don't worry, Devi. You're an iron man. We are proud of you,' he said.

I met the negotiators and a few Indian Airlines officials. Three or four buses were waiting. All the passengers were ferried to the A320 and the Boeing 737, which were standing a distance away from the A300. I told the negotiators that the plane had to be checked thoroughly. Chief had told me there was a bomb.

I was to fly back on the A320 with my crew and about half the passengers. It looked amazingly beautiful; it was our own plane flown by our crew. The ladder was missing though: Kandahar airport had one ladder. The A320 crew was on the plane. They waved at us. When the ladder was fixed, they came down. 'Congratulations,' they kept saying. Captain Rao was carrying his satellite phone. My telephone batteries were weak, and I requested him for his. But he had no batteries.

I was still standing on the tarmac when Jaswant Singh came along. He was accompanied by the Taliban foreign minister.

'Come and meet Jaswant Singh,' Captain Suri said. 'This is Captain Sharan, sir. He was the flight commander,' he said, introducing me.

I also met Mr Muttawakil.

Then it was time to get on the A320. Boarding passes were distributed. I, the commander of the hijacked A300, would now be a passenger. I was seated in the first row, my boarding card A1. The passengers were filing in, ready to go home. Our story was coming to an end, and there was little for me to do except rejoice that all my passengers, except for Ripin Katyal, were safe. Jaswant Singh and the Taliban foreign minister also came aboard. The latter had an interpreter: I don't think he understood much English.

A little later, Mr Singh called for me. He was in the galley. After we shook hands again and he congratulated me, I took out the night-vision binoculars and handed it over. I explained where they came from.

'I hope there isn't a bomb in it,' he said.

Mr Singh now wanted to head home. 'The people are waiting for us in New Delhi. Let's leave now,' he said.

I went back and sat down. Next to me sat Rajinder. It was almost like the old days!

A short while into the flight, I received fresh summons. The external affairs minister wanted to speak to me again. 'Tell me about Amritsar. What happened?' he asked.

'There were no security arrangements. Everything was delayed. Even the bowser didn't come on time...' I told him the whole story. He listened quietly but didn't say much.

The journey back to New Delhi took about an hour and forty minutes. It was one of the happiest flights of my life. The smiles were back; the passengers were tired, but relieved. There has never been so much laughter on any journey. The brotherhood would remain. I saw people exchanging addresses and telephone numbers. I tried to meet as many passengers as I could.

My only remaining worry was the notorious Delhi fog. How terrible it will be if we can't land because of the fog. The plane would have to be diverted and our relatives would have spent all those hours in the airport waiting for us, I thought. It made the evening more special as this was the millennium eve. I truly comprehended what a wonderful gift freedom is.

The plane finally landed. Mr Jaswant Singh got off and so did the negotiators. It was my turn. I took one step and I could see hundreds of media people at the airport. I spotted the civil aviation minister, Sharad Yadav, and heavy industries and public enterprises minister, Manohar Joshi. The Delhi chief minister, Ms. Sheila Dixit, was also there. As I got off, I first hugged Captain D. Kalia, a colleague, and several members of the Indian Commercial Pilots' Association. I was laughing. I was crying. I was still not on the tarmac; there were people on the ladder congratulating me.

Finally, I was on terra firma. 'Thank you, God,' I said silently, my lips moving slightly.

The three ministers greeted me. Another much respected flight commander and friend, Captain R.S. Dhillon, ran over. He hugged me and wouldn't let me go. It was an emotional moment. Finally, he took my flight bag.

'Please let me carry my bag,' I told him.

'No, you won't.'

I saw a million flashbulbs popping, the cameras following me as I walked. It was a heady feeling. My crew also got down. What a reception it was! All the officials and hundreds, no, thousands of people, were waiting to greet us. As I walked through the green channel, the people there were standing up. '*Aaj sab kuch maaf hain.* (We won't check anything today),' one of them said.

Then there were the flowers. The ministers had given me bouquets; as had some civilian aviation people including my flight engineers, Mr Sethi and Mr A.K. Gupta, and other colleagues.

All this while, I was looking around. I wanted to see my family. There were a lot of familiar faces, but not my wife. And then I saw her. She was walking towards me. She was wearing a pink salwar kameez and those pearls. I have never seen her looking so beautiful before. She hadn't forgotten even after those seven terrible days. We embraced and my eyes were wet. I realized I was home. My mother had come too, as had my brother and my buddy, Captain S.S. Virk.

Then I had 'taken off' again. They lifted me up and carried me to the car. Is this what they called a hero's welcome? I thought. Was I a hero?

There wasn't much more time to think. Everything was a wonderful blur. Happiness all around, pure joy and relief! I was back, with my friends and my family. I was home.

The terror of Amritsar and Lahore, of Dubai and Kandahar were history. It was finally over.

The media crowded around, their cameras trained, but my friends literally dumped me into our Maruti Omni.

I had been looking for my children. I was hoping they wouldn't be lost in the mayhem. They, along with my sister in-law, Jasneet and my friend, Hardeep Singh, were in the car. 'Let's get out of here before the media swarms all over us,' I said.

Hardeep started the car, and we were away.

My children embraced me, and I held them tightly in my arms in the speeding car. I hadn't shaved for eight days or even brushed my teeth properly. But I had to hold them. They were crying. They didn't know whether I would come back. I couldn't hold back the tears either. 'I am sorry I spoiled your holidays. I couldn't take you to Sharjah,' I told them.

A Delhi Police vehicle was following our car. When we reached the Indian Airlines housing colony at Vasant Vihar, a policeman got off and stood at attention.

'Sir, can we go in?'

'Of course.'

He need not have followed us. The hijackers were in Kandahar!

As I got out of the car, I noticed the entire colony, several hundred people at least were waiting outside my building. '*Bharat Mata ki jai*,' a group of boys shouted as I got out. I met everyone there. There were a lot of media people taking photographs.

Many of my friends were at home. The living room was full of flowers. Navneet had arranged an impromptu party. After all the handshaking and backslapping, I noticed something: no one was asking me anything about the hijacking.

'Don't you want to know what happened?' I asked someone.

'Not now. You're so tired. We'll discuss this when you're more relaxed.'

As I sat there with everyone looking at me, I remembered how far I had travelled, how my life had changed since I had last been here before flying to Kathmandu on Christmas Eve. I was finally home with my family. It felt like much longer than that.

What do you do then?

Someone pulled out a bottle of Johnnie Walker Black Label whisky. There were a lot of laddoos. Someone put on music. I think we danced all night.

In the prevailing joy, few noticed how the government's arrangements at the airport for receiving the passengers and crew were inadequate. The medical team sat idle as the passengers and crew left. They did not know what to do and there was nobody to guide them. Sharad Yadav's address could not be heard as there were no microphones and worse, senior policemen left as soon as the Delhi lieutenant-governor, Vijay Kapoor, and the chief minister, Sheila Dixit, left. Even an hour after the flight landed, there were IC 814 passengers wandering around the airport; there weren't enough cars to take them home.

In one home in Gurgaon, there was no rejoicing. When Rachna Katyal returned late in the evening, she found the entire family assembled. But her husband was missing.

Where was he? She was told he was injured and receiving treatment. And she couldn't see him. She refused to believe anyone. She wanted to see him. She wanted to know why everyone else was present. Even on the plane, she had suspected the worst had happened.

When Rachna was finally screaming in frustration and demanding to know, the doctors told the family to tell her, even though the initial plan had been to keep it a secret for a while.

At 2.30 a.m., when she heard, she broke down immediately and went into a state of shock. She was under sedation for several days.

My ordeal in Kandahar, the seven days and nights in the A300 with the hijackers was over; I had left behind my friends, Captain S.P.S. Suri and Captain Rao, and of course, my plane. At the best of times, a night in Taliban-held Kandahar wasn't going to be easy; the rogues at the airport had no time for my friends. Where would they spend New Year's Eve? I was finally at home with my wife and daughters. So were most of the crew and the passengers. There were no rooms for Suri, Rao, Nagar and two other Indian Airlines staffers at the airport; they'd been allotted to the guest of honor, Maulana Masood Azhar, and the two terrorists handed over by the Indian government and of course, the hijackers.

As I left for New Delhi, I had told them about the '*tohfa* (gift)' the hijackers had for all of India in the bulk hold of the plane. '*Hamara commander bolta hain hum tumhe nahin jaane denge jab tak isme se hamara ek tohfa nahin utaroge* (My commanders had ordered me not to let you go till I get the gift out of the plane),' one of the hijackers told Suri. 'They would have taken all kinds of valuables—watches, jewelry and cash—from the passengers. That's probably lying in the cabin. And that's what they want,' thought Suri.

Instead, the hijackers forced Suri to check—it contained the RDX. If they hadn't got Masood Azhar back, they would have blown up the plane on New Year's Eve. That would have been their gift to India. Captain Suri remembers the 'loud boom' at the far end of the airport, after the hijackers took away the 'tohfa.' That's what happened to the RDX meant for the plane.

I had spent seven nights in Kandahar, in the plane, of course. Suri and Rao couldn't manage that; the stench in the A300 was by then, terrible. With no rooms available, they were forced to spend the night lying outside, next to a bonfire. A Taliban leader walked over as they lay there, shivering, the cold almost unbearable. '*Sardar, badaam kha le. Raat kut jayega*. (Have some almonds. You'll manage. It'll soon be dawn.)' he told Suri.

They were in the A300 cockpit anyway, the next morning, despite warnings by the air-traffic controller. They were not to take off. They didn't have permission. The plane's battery almost dead, they, after a quick prayer, started one engine. Waheguru had heard Suri's prayers; the engine, almost miraculously, came to life. 'When we were taxiing, we started the second engine. The air-traffic controller in Kandahar kept telling us, even warning us. He said we did not have permission to take off but take off we did. We didn't want permission from the Taliban to go home,' Suri told me. Their call sign IC 814(D), they heard from the Pakistan ATC; they didn't have clearance to fly over Pakistan. Nevertheless, they did fly over Pakistan: it's only a few minutes and soon they were entering Indian airspace. It's then that the Indian Air Force flight controller came on. 'You are cleared straight for Delhi,' the flight controller said. 'Welcome home!'

Chapter Twelve

The NSG commandos couldn't get near Captain Sharan's plane in Amritsar on Christmas Eve. Nor could they attempt a rescue in Dubai or Kandahar. As the negotiators sat with the hijackers and the Taliban, and the impatient spoke of commando operations, many remembered a thrilling yesterday, when almost everything came right. It was at Entebbe.

'India is not Israel, nor do I think that as yet any of our commando units is capable of repeating the uniquely spectacular Entebbe rescue operation by the Israeli commando group Sayaret Matkal,' says Arun Mukherjee, former director-general of police, West Bengal. When a group of Burmese rebels had hijacked a Thai Airways plane to Calcutta in November 1990, Mukherjee had played a key role in the rescue operations.

In a letter to Brajesh Mishra, on 10 January 2000, he makes several telling points about the shortcomings in the way in which the hijacking of IC 814 was handled and suggests some measures to improve the CMG's poor legwork. Mukherjee cites his own experience in Calcutta. Initial decisions, he says, were taken at the local level, long before the CMG got together. The hijacked plane was parked in the VIP bay of Dum Dum Airport. The area was so well-lit that it almost blinded the hijackers. It had the additional advantage that it could be effectively cordoned off and normal traffic not disrupted. Also, preliminary negotiations between the hijackers began before the CMG hotline was activated, and he and the state home secretary, Manish Gupta gradually established rapport with the hijackers. They won their confidence and gradually wore them down, which led to their eventual surrender.

Mukherjee believes his exposure to available literature on the hijacking and his 'equations' with CMG officials in New Delhi, as a result of his stints as a director of the CBI and in the Home Ministry, were a great help.

Among the shortcomings in the airlines and government procedures Mukherjee points out:

- Nearly two hundred passengers passed through the security check in twenty minutes, just another example of the extremely lax security arrangements at Kathmandu. 'Weren't our Indian Airlines staff required to keep an eye on the security checks and make some checks on their own before a passenger was allowed to board our plane? A more precise cross-checking system by the Air India and Indian Airlines staff is called for at all points. There should also be more stringent periodic security vetting of our staff.'
- There is no anti-hijacking training program for pilots and crew, and no guidelines for the passengers. Mukherjee speaks of finding ways to form small groups amongst passengers to resist the hijackers, if necessary. That Captain Sharan had

made similar efforts halfway through his ordeal suggests that such efforts are viable.

- Airlines should prepare a series of short, coded messages so the pilot or other crew members can convey to the air traffic controller information about the number of hijackers and the kind of weapons they are carrying without arousing the slightest suspicion among the hijackers. Sharan did send one such message. But had there been a more codified system, the ambiguity about the amount of fuel he was carrying would not have arisen.
- Mukherjee calls for the creation of a media management group and a separate organization to deal with the family members of the hostages. It is important 'to educate the media and public about the nation's policy in dealing with hijackers and what should be appropriate government responses. The December 1999 episode was marked by the absence of any forethought or preparation on these counts.'
- Mukherjee also speaks of the NSG failure during the Thai Airways hijacking. 'We were told that the NSG commandos would reach Calcutta within two hours. The group landed at Calcutta after about three hours.' After landing, the NSG group wanted to take their plane next to the hijacked one to 'facilitate commando action'. 'We felt this could make the hijackers jittery and provoke them to resort to retaliatory action against the hostages. I explained the situation to the CMG, and they agreed with us that the NSG plane must not go near the hijacked one at that stage... The leader of the NSG team (an army officer) came for a briefing by us about the developments. He did not appear to be well-versed in the niceties and imperatives of the negotiation process and kept asking how long we proposed to go on talking with the hijackers and when he could mount his assault on the

hijacked plane! We had to fall back on the CMG, and they directed that no raid should begin till it was okayed by them in consultation with us. Though it took us a couple of hours more, the outcome was like a bloodless coup. The hijackers surrendered to us in the manner proposed by us and without any hostage being harmed.' He expresses the hope that the 'skill and competence of our commando groups have improved substantially over the last nine years'.

- 'It would be desirable to think of incapacitating disabling/disorienting the hijackers by drugging them through food and beverages. Biochemical, biomedical and other experts may be asked to conduct experiments.'
- Certain airports should be designated as vulnerable and special precautions taken there. Several airports in the east and north-east like Bagdogra, Guwahati, Silchar, Kohima, Imphal and Agartala should be included in the list of vulnerable airports.
- Preparations for the simultaneous handling of the hijacking of two or three planes should be made. Mukherjee believes this is a distinct possibility and setting up additional CMGs and allied groups in adjacent groups and positioning several commando units at selected locations to reduce response times should be made. 'Mock-exercises to deal with multiple hijackings should also be organized periodically.' And the location of the CMG headquarters should be a well-guarded secret.
- A joint team of IB, RAW and CBI officials should prepare a compulsory reading list for CMG members and other groups after consulting experts. The IB and RAW should study all previous hijacking incidents closely. 'I presume there are such studies based on official reports. Many more unstated details and suggestions may emerge if steps are taken to

closely interview the persons had handed such episodes as CMG and its allied group members, commandos, airport officials, cockpit and cabin crew.'

- For those who have suggested that the aircraft should have been stopped at Raja Sansi Airport even if that meant the death of a few more passengers, Mukherjee has only scorn. 'What could be the number of a "few more?" Ten, twenty, fifty? Could our national psyche accept this an "inescapable sacrifice"? Haven't we seen how hysterical we can become even at the death of just one of the passengers?' he asks. That does not stop him from vehemently criticizing the authorities for the Amritsar fiasco. It 'will continue to be a sad reflection on our level of preparedness both at New Delhi and Amritsar, more so when we knew that as many as five hijacked planes had earlier landed at Amritsar. The gross deficiency must be rectified at the earliest... We may devise some means of utilizing Amritsar as a trap for hijacked planes.'
- In his paper, 'Terrorism, Institutional Collapse and Emergency Response Protocols', K.P.S. Gill, who foiled two hijackings at Amritsar, virtually taking on the hijackers personally (on 27 March and 24 April 1993) outlined several reasons for the failures at Raja Sansi Airport.
- The inability to establish an unambiguous center of command within reasonable time and reasonably in such a crisis is to be measured in minutes, not hours, was the first and most significant failure. The existing emergency response systems are inadequate. The 'abdication of responsibility by the majority of those who are required to act' was evidence of this inadequacy, and this was played out through 'the great charade' committee work. The committees discuss, communicate and manage but refuse to take decisive action.

- Those who 'took charge, did not know what was to be done. Each began... trying to reinvent the wheel, with no guidelines, no reference to a historical context and no structured system of emergency response.'

  'There was no clear line of communication and conflicting, and contradictory instructions were received through random and informal modes of communication, including cell phones.'

  'No system for providing adequate technical backup to decision-makers was in place till the end of the crisis. Simple but critical calculations, such as the available fuel in the plane had clearly not been made. Nor were the technical and military options for immobilizing the plane adequately clarified or explored. Individuals from non-technical backgrounds with limited or no prior experience either of a crisis of this kind, or of other aviation or military emergency were evidently wracking their brains to figure out some sort of solution.'
- There is no national policy on hostage or hijacking situations or on terrorism that could provide guidelines to resolve such a crisis.
- The rapid deployment forces in New Delhi failed to reach the airport on time and the security men at the airport and in Amritsar lacked the capabilities the NSG had.
- The hijackers' claim, articulated through the pilot, that they were armed with AK-47s was accepted as gospel and hastily communicated to every journalist in the vicinity... This perception had a powerful impact, not only on those who were charged with decision-making in this crisis, but also on our relations with a friendly country.
- India heaped ignominy on Nepal and arbitrarily suspended flights. A breach had occurred, but nevertheless the

response was disproportionate. 'I cannot conceive of a less diplomatically sound course of action. Worse still, each element of this disgracing of Nepal was carried out in public.'

- There was no coordinated media response, and senior officials made conflicting statements. There needed to be more professionalism in the handling of these areas.
- The Indian government's handling of the relatives of the hijacked passengers was similarly inept. Poor media management, the contradictory and exaggerated official statements 'fed the hysteria of the relatives.'

The government had failed, was Gill's assessment. He speaks of 'loss of control, of confusion and impotence,' and 'the proliferation of manifestly puerile statements. and of empty political rhetoric posturing as policy'.

'Put yourself in the hijackers' place, and that of their sponsors, and try to imagine the sense of empowerment and satisfaction. It is not just of securing the release of three militants, but of having discomfited and even humiliated so many senior Indian leaders including ministers and perhaps the prime minister himself.'

The glaring shortcomings in the way that the episode was handled become more evident when one compares it to the way that the hijacking at Entebbe was dealt with. There are similarities between the two hijackings which drive home the contrast. Five terrorists hijacked Captain Sharan's A300; four had commandeered the Air France A300B. IC 814 reached Kandahar via Lahore and Al Minhad; AF-139 got to Entebbe in faraway Uganda via Benghazi. Ugandan president Idi Amin collaborated with the hijackers, who were Palestinian guerrillas and terrorists of the German Baader-Meinhof gang. The Taliban weren't precisely hostile to the hijackers; later Jaswant Singh confirmed that the Afghan government had helped the latter.

At Entebbe, the demand had been for the release of fifty-three imprisoned terrorists. The hijackers at Kandahar wanted thirty-five imprisoned terrorists released. Both sets of hijackers used the customary pistols and grenades, and both wanted money: the ones at Entebbe, US $5 million and at Kandahar, US $200 million.

The contrast in the outcome could not be starker. At Kandahar, the hijackers escaped, and the Indian government was forced to release three terrorists. On the other hand, every terrorist died at Entebbe and all of Israel rejoiced.

The Enebbe operation has been called a victory of training and superior tactics. Just after the Israeli government learned about the hijacking, on 27 June 1976, the Sayeret Matkal commandos were placed on alert. The hijackers released passengers who did not have Israeli passports, leaving behind the Israelis and the Air France crew, who elected to stay with the Israelis. The terrorists initially said the hostages would be executed from 1 July if their demands were not met. The deadline was later extended to 4 July. From the released passengers, the Israelis quickly learned about the airport's layout and the defenses. They learned that the Ugandans were cooperating fully with the hijackers. An Israeli security man who was formerly stationed at Entebbe provided 8 mm film footage of the airport.

While the Israeli cabinet decided on the operation, the commandos started preparing for the mission. They practised getting off a plane and hitting the tarmac and pulverizing all opposition. Then, after the Rabin government cleared the plan, the C-130 Hercules planes carrying the commandos took off from Israel, heading in different directions initially to confuse potential spies and flying low to avoid detection by Soviet ships and Egyptian radar. After a brief stop for refueling, the C-130s continued south towards Entebbe.

It was 11 p.m. (Israeli time) when the lead aircraft touched down behind a hillock a little distance away from the old terminal where the hostages were being held. First out of the plane was a black Mercedes-Benz, like one that President Amin had. The president had come to the airport several times in such a car. The Israelis thought it would confuse the Ugandan soldiers, winning them a few precious seconds. Two Land Rovers followed. All the vehicles flew Ugandan flags, and the commandos were dressed in Ugandan military uniforms.

The vehicles cruised towards the terminals with their lights on, at about 40 mph. After a minute's drive, two Ugandan guards challenged the Israelis. The Israelis slowed down as if they were stopping and then opened fire.

They shot both guards with their silenced Berettas but not before one of the Ugandans fired, the burst of the automatic rifle ripping through the night.

The Israelis couldn't count on taking anyone by surprise anymore. As they parked outside the terminal, a terrorist ran inside yelling, 'The Ugandans have gone crazy. They are shooting at us!'

Within three minutes of the landing, four of the terrorists were killed. (The initial four hijackers had been joined by others.) The commandos shot two of the terrorists whom the freed passengers had described, and a woman terrorist. A commando shot the fourth before he fired his AK-47.

The commando team saw two men in the VIP lounge in the terminal but didn't fire till they saw one of them wearing a grenade belt. He dropped a grenade, but both terrorists were shot dead. All the terrorists were now killed, but the Ugandans still had to be fought off. A sniper fired from the nearby control tower at the Israeli commando leader, Lieutenant-Colonel Jonathan Netanyahu, mortally wounding him. Seconds later, one of the four Israeli armored personnel carriers fired rockets at the tower and, as one report said, 'the top of the building disappeared in a blinding explosion'.

Within only fifteen minutes of the first C-130 landing, the hostages were freed, and the area secured. Despite the passengers being in shock or hysterical, and the difficulties in getting an accurate headcount, less than an hour after the first C-130 landed, a plane took off with over a hundred rescued hostages.

The other commandos retreated behind the screen of smoke bombs and timed explosive devices, but not after they destroyed some Ugandan MiG fighters (eight according to one report, eleven according to another) parked on the tarmac. The rescue operations took just over an hour and a half. The leader of the commando operation, Lieutenant-Colonel Netanyahu, was killed as was at least one hostage, an elderly lady, who had been taken to a local hospital and was not present during the operation. She was executed by the Idi Amin regime. But the others, after a brief refueling stop at Nairobi, were back in Israel.

Chief and his men hijacked Captain Sharan's A300 on 24 December. Five years earlier, on the same day, a suicide squad of the Algerian Armed Islamic Group boarded an Air France Airbus Flight 8969 at Algiers, disguised as airport security men and just before take-off, produced miniature Kalashnikov assault rifles with collapsible stacks. The 257 passengers and crew were their prisoners.

As Martin Arostegui writes in *The Twilight Warriors* (St. Martin's Press), the hijackers wanted to be flown to Paris. They planned to blow up the aircraft in mid-air over the Eiffel Tower. This would be their moment of glory. And they meant business. For, minutes after taking over the Airbus, they dragged an Algerian policeman and a Vietnamese diplomat to the front of the aircraft and despite their cries for mercy, shot them and dumped the bodies on the tarmac. In Paris and Algiers, the crises management teams gathered. The French GIGN (super gendarmes) flew south on an Air France Airbus identical to the hijacked plane. On the flight, they familiarized themselves with the aircraft's workings, and planned and practised their counter-hijack operation. In Paris, French prime minister, Édouard Balladur and the foreign and interior ministers got together with Philippe Legorjus, chief security consultant of Air France. By now, the hijackers wanted to fly to Marseilles, but the Algerian authorities, especially the army's commandos, the Ninjas, wouldn't agree to this. The gendarmes wanted to use explosives to blast their way inside the plane, but the French government did not give permission. They remembered a similar operation when Egyptian commandos had tried to storm an Egyptair plane, and fifty-nine hostages had died in the attempt.

As the French and Algerian governments conferred, the hijackers announced on Christmas Day that they would start killing hostages every half hour. At 9.30 p.m., they brought a young cook employed at the French Embassy at Algiers to the cockpit. 'If you don't allow the plane to take off, they are going to kill me,' he pleaded over the radio.

French efforts to intervene were in vain. The Algerians refused to let the plane fly off, probably certain the terrorists weren't going to shoot anyone. Half an hour later, the cook's body was on the tarmac.

Later that night, the Algerians let the plane fly to Marseilles, where the French cleared it to land. The French commandos, waiting at the Spanish airport of Palma de Mallorca, took off and landed just twenty minutes before the hijackers with their hostages at Marseilles, using an airstrip adjacent to the main airport. By the time the hijacked plane landed, the commando snipers were ready at the control tower and paratroopers were waiting in the tall grass beside the runway.

The hijackers wanted twenty-seven tons of fuel, far more than necessary. At one point during the discussions, the hijackers' leader Abdul Yahia shouted into the cockpit microphone, 'You want us to blow up everything right here? You have one and a half hours to let us take off to Paris.'

The hijackers had fitted explosives on the plane after landing at Marseilles at 3.30 a.m. Two ten-stick packs of dynamite had been placed in the cockpit and beneath a row of seats. They were fused by one detonator. (The hijackers at Kandahar also had explosives on board, as Jaswant Singh later announced.)

The negotiators at Marseilles offered the hijackers food and sent in janitors to clean the stinking toilets. The stewards and service crew fitted tiny microphone and infra-red close circuit cameras in the plane. The negotiators thus knew the entrances to the plane were not booby-trapped and that two terrorists were always inside the cockpit.

At midday, the hijackers made their last concession, letting off an elderly couple. They reported that the hijackers were growing increasingly impatient and irritable and were reading out passages from the Koran. (Doctor in Kandahar had made similar proselytizing efforts.)

By late afternoon, the French commandos started preparing themselves with the necessary bullet-proof gear and weapons, revolvers, sub-machine guns and automatic pistols. Snipers took aim at the cockpit.

Just before 5 p.m., as the commandos were ready for assault, the plane which had been parked four hundred yards away, began to move slowly towards the control tower. Yahia announced that he would act if the plane was not refueled in fifteen minutes. As in Amritsar, the negotiators said the refueling trucks were on their way. The commandos repositioned themselves.

At a predetermined signal from Captain Denis de Favier, who headed the operation, the commandos moved the mobile ladder towards the plane and a sniper fired six rounds into the cockpit to distract the terrorists.

As the gendarmes entered the aircraft after throwing a stun grenade inside, they surprised two hijackers making for the cockpit. They shot one but the other entered the cockpit to warn Yahia and the other hijacker who were holed up there, along with the crew. Instantly, the gendarmes were at the receiving end of a hail of AK-47 bullets. De Favier, who led the first assault, reported that 'Six of my men fell wounded around me as we came inside. The terrorists were highly trained and very quick. They hardly took a second between releasing spent ammunition clips and inserting fresh ones... They knew exactly how to fire.' A second wave of gendarmes entered, attracting fire even before they entered the aircraft.

While the hijackers were thus occupied, security men evacuated the 159 passengers, sliding them out on escape chutes from the back of the plane. Stray bullets flew around them but only thirteen of the passengers had to be treated for light injuries, mostly cuts and bruises. The evacuation took only twenty minutes.

Meanwhile the battle raged on in front. The cockpit area was rapidly becoming a killing ground. Gendarmes continued to aim at the sections of the partition through which the gunfire was coming. After about ten minutes of fighting, the gendarmes heard the pilot's voice. 'Stop shooting,' he shouted.

They entered the cockpit to find the dead terrorists, the unscathed cabin crew and the dynamite beneath the pilot's seat. The terrorists hadn't had time to operate the fuse-box mechanisms and blow up the plane. The terrorists aboard Air France Flight 8969 were probably better trained than Chief and his men, and certainly better armed.

Nine gendarmes were seriously injured in the gun-battle. A daring rescue operation was carried out by the Special Air Service when a Lufthansa aircraft was hijacked in October 1977 to Dubai and Mogadishu, Somalia. After the plane landed at Mogadishu airport, the terrorists tossed out the pilot's dead body. The hijackers wanted the release of members of the Baader-Meinhof gang. The rescue operation, says William Seymour in British Special Forces (Sidgwick & Jackson), was planned by the SAS and German commandos. When the two SAS men flung percussion grenades from each side of the aircraft, the Germans bashed in the emergency doors and entered the cabin. Bullets hummed over the heads of the seventy-nine passengers still strapped in their seats and two grenades exploded below the seats. Miraculously, the passengers and crew were not hurt. Three terrorists were killed and one arrested.

All hijackings haven't ended so successfully. A daring Abu Nidal–inspired operation that ended in bloodshed was the September 1986 hijack at Karachi airport. This is described by Yossi Melman in *The Master Terrorist: The True Story behind Abu Nidal* (Sidgwick & Jackson). The Pan Am 747 was on the tarmac when four hijackers drove up to the plane dressed as security men, seized the plane and demanded that the New York–bound plane be flown to Cyprus. When the lights dimmed and the air conditioning shut off because there was no fuel, the gunmen panicked and began shooting wildly and lobbing grenades inside the cabin. Fourteen of the 389 passengers, a member of the crew and a ground staffer died, and about a hundred others were injured.

A year earlier, in November 1985, there was another Abu Nidal–inspired hijack of an Egyptair Athens-Cairo flight to

Valletta, Malta. Fifty-nine people died in the rescue operations and ten were wounded.

Like Chief and his men, other hijackers have also got away. A BA flight from London in November 1974 was hijacked to Dubai and then flown to Tunis. A West German passenger was killed and after lengthy negotiations, most of the other passengers and crew were freed, but the hijackers permitted to fly off to Libya. A KLM flight to Tokyo in November 1973 was hijacked over Iraq and taken to Nicosia, Cyprus, and then to Valletta, Malta. Eventually the hijackers were permitted to fly to Syria.

The Israeli rescue operation in Entebbe came eight days after the hijacking; the passengers of IC 814, except Ripin Katyal, were returned in exchange for three terrorists after eight days too. There have been longer stand-offs: Palestinian terrorists had released their last hostages forty days after they hijacked an El Al flight to Algiers in July 1968. And when Shiite gunmen seized a TWA Boeing, forcing the pilot to fly to Beirut, they held thirty-nine Americans for eighteen days before the Syrians brought about their release.

'Eight days is a long time when you don't know if you're going to live or die,' says Ashok Kathuria, a passenger on IC 814.

Could the Indian government have done an Entebbe at Kandahar? After all, Indian commandos were sitting in the aircraft there.

'I am aware of Entebbe. I don't think the government is capable of such action. It was completely helpless during the crisis. They had no information. There was impotence. How can they do what the Israelis did?' asks Kathuria.

Epilogue

Every day with the hijackers was a like a ride on a roller coaster. One thought the end was there a hundred times every day. But then there would be moments when there was rising hope.

How did we survive?

When I look back at those difficult nights and days, guns pointed at us, grenades with the pins pulled out, fanatical hijackers to whom blowing up the plane in mid-air was merely a grand gesture with no thought of the human tragedy involved, I realize that only patience and teamwork saved us. Our refusal to get into arguments with the hijackers and our efforts to get on with them probably saved our lives. If we had turned aggressive or tried to confront them, they might have killed us all. While we were prepared to take them on should they have started randomly killing us, I am glad we did not try confronting them before that It wouldn't have been very heroic; it would have been foolhardy.

The death of Ripin Katyal was terrible but I am so grateful that no one else was killed. As a flight commander, my job is to fly a plane from Place A to Place B. But in the situation I found myself in, my responsibilities were far greater. We are not trained for such emergencies, so everything we did was by instinct. I felt that it was my duty to try to save the passengers, and I tried to do my duty honestly, sincerely and to the best of my ability. I tried to figure out rapidly what were the best moves to make. For example, I tried hard to bring about the landing in Amritsar, to give Indian authorities a chance to organize a commando operation. The hijackers weren't very happy that I had landed in Amritsar, and they mentioned that during the days in Kandahar.

I am thankful I didn't reduce myself to a shivering wreck or lose my head after the guns and grenades came out. And I am glad that my courage never failed. There were some opportunities after the hijacking for me and the cockpit crew to escape, well, probably escape, but we didn't take advantage of these opportunities. I felt I had to stay on the plane with my passengers, they were depending on me, they were looking towards me for guidance. It was an awesome responsibility.

The nightmare is over, but the memories will not go away. And one reason is a video sent to me by one of the passengers. There is something fascinating about the video—I don't want to watch it and then, I want to. It doesn't show the actual hijacking, but it has the moments before and after, from the duty-free shop at Kathmandu airport and IC 814 taking off, and then from the time the hijackers left to our return journey. It begins in the red brick airport with the passengers in light parkas and golf caps walking around, posing for the hand-held camera, the duty-free shop and the airport bar behind them. Then, appearing briefly on the screen, there is a young man in a grey jacket and a blue backpack, tall and slim, always with his back to the camera. He looked familiar at once and after a moment, it all came back. It was probably Bhola! Just to watch him walking around still gives me the creeps.

I sometimes wonder how the passenger could film so much video footage. There are shots of people, jerky and at times unfocused, of passengers on the tarmac, two women posing for last-minute shots, and then, clambering onto the plane. There's a close-up of the instructions for technicians about the plane's weight: 'Empty 81,229; Maximum weight 142,000.' Then, we are inside the plane, bathed in the yellow light, still in the age of innocence. Everyone is happy, waving as the camera pans. I recognized Christina and Roberto at the back, and many others.

Then, the camera is focused outside the windowpane, at the Royal Nepal Airlines plane on the tarmac, before our plane begins moving. Even the moment of take-off is so clear. How did we allow someone to operate a video camera inside a moving plane?

There's nothing of the hijacking. The hijackers had confiscated all the film, but apparently the man who took this video had given them an empty cassette instead. But the first moments of freedom are all there. You can hear the chattering in the cabins, see the cars parked outside and the faces, all the faces. Stubbly, grimy faces. Everyone smiling and waving, shaking hands, hugging each other as if their lives depended on it. It's quite a home-movie. There's the purser, waving to the cameras and a lot of other passengers and then, in a long shot, standing at the door, yours truly. I am surprised my tunic looks so well pressed. I am posing for the shot.

'Kindly send me a copy,' I shout. And then there's a moment of embarrassment. A man in a checked shirt and golf cap, stocky and dark, walks up to me and hugs me. He kisses me and kisses me again. And a moment later, he kisses me a third time. All on the cheek, thank God!

The women are laughing and as the camera pans frenetically, I see my 177 friends exuberant after being under the iron control of the hijackers for a week. There's a bit of anger; a young boy in a yellow parka is saying, '*Goli maar dunga usko*. (I'll shoot him.)' It is obviously a reference to the hijackers. It seemed a bit strange, a flash of anger when there is so much laughter and so many hugs.

Then we're getting off the plane. Another jerky pan and I remembered the knot of cars and buses around the plane, the white and black turbans of the Taliban. In the background, far, far away stands a solitary tank, a little menacing but who cares? Everyone's going home. There are shots of us getting off the plane and into a bus. We're on the plane going home and Jaswant Singh arrives, in a dark green jacket, shaking hands. And then, he's gone, the nightmare is over, the tape has run out...

This cassette didn't have the worst parts; it didn't have anything of the bad days.

As a pilot, I am responsible for my passengers' safety and a hijacking is the ultimate test of one's presence of mind and responses. I had hoped this was the last hijacking that ever happened but there was one almost immediately after, and that too an Afghan airline! I always feel terrible for the innocent passengers who get involved. For us, the crew, in a sense, it is an uncommon but inherent risk associated with our work. But I always feel terrible for the passengers.

Of the passengers, there were many who shrugged off the hijacking. 'They were terrible moments; there were so many times when I thought I wouldn't make it out of the plane,' said Ashok Kathuria.

There was fear of flying again, but even that had to be overcome. 'On 31 January, I had to go to Kathmandu, and I did,' said Khurana.

Months after the hijacking, many passengers remained bitter about the attitude of the airlines management. 'Captain Sharan has won the Conway Safe Skies Award. Well, it takes a foreign country to acknowledge courage and ability. The attitude of the airlines management has been indifference.'

'I think there is no value for human life in this country,' said Ramesh Grover. 'I haven't even got a letter of acknowledgement from Indian Airlines!'

Once the passengers were back, the government could stand up and accuse Pakistan. To an extent, Jaswant Singh remained diplomatic when he maintained that there were 'sufficient' indications of Pakistani involvement. The hijackers, he said, took 'breaks' during the negotiations and consulted 'others.' They were not the Taliban. The hijackers and the three freed militants had left for Quetta, the Pakistani city closest to Kandahar. And of course, he continued to deny that India had 'suddenly become a soft state'.

But while the foreign minister only talked covertly about Pakistani involvement, Brajesh Mishra was far more open. 'The Pakistan establishment is responsible for it... All evidence and intercepts we have suggested this. One such intercept showed that one militant outfit in Jammu and Kashmir asked another in the state why it condemned the hijack. The other replied it got the instructions from Pakistan.' The hijackers were mainly Pakistani nationals and thirty-three of the thirty-six militants they wanted released were Pakistani. L.K. Advani, the home minister, also made similar statements.

The evidence behind such charges is quite substantial. Indian government officials believe that Asam Saboor, an official at the Pakistan Embassy in Kathmandu, a senior Pakistani diplomat and another Pakistani, Zia Ansari, had aided the hijackers.

Saboor was later sent back from Nepal for activities unusual for a diplomat.

A Pakistan Embassy car (42 CD 14) arrived at the airport just before IC 814 took off from Kathmandu and the three officials proceeded to the departure lounge. They handed a bag to the would-be hijackers. It presumably contained the hand grenades and pistols. One of these three officials had apparently supplied RDX to militants several years ago.

The idea of Pakistani involvement was also reinforced by the fact that the freed militants found refuge there, though Pakistan's foreign minister, Abdus Sattar, stated that such speculation was 'baseless and false'. The hijackers were not Pakistani and if they did enter Pakistan, they would 'be arrested and made to face charges. I can say with full responsibility they have not entered Pakistan,' he said.

Maulana Masood Azhar himself showed such denials to be meaningless when he stated in Karachi in January 2000 that the other two freed militants were, like him, in Pakistan. They had driven out of Kandahar airport with the hijackers but after about half an hour, the hijackers had switched vehicles, freed their Taliban hostage and told the Maulana they were returning to India. The three militants, including the Maulana returned to Pakistan.

Moreover, the Maulana's return to active politics, unhampered in any way by Pakistani authorities, also shows their tacit support for his cause. Later in January, his speech outside a Karachi mosque about 'Muslims not resting in peace until America and India are destroyed' evoked a strong response from the US. 'We hold the Pakistan government responsible for Masood's actions, which threaten the lives of our citizens... We find Masood's speech deplorable and his reported remarks about destroying America and India unacceptable,' said a government spokesman.

Investigation into the hijacking continued, spearheaded by the CBI's special investigation team. In Mumbai, police arrested Suresh Bhatnate, owner of Seven Travels and his two employees Prakash Jadhav and Vishnu Yeram for providing fake Indian passports to four ISI agents for the hijackers. They also found two AK-56 assault rifles, arms and ammunition. The passports were used by two of the hijackers, including Chief. They were genuine passports, obtained by using forged documents—school-leaving certificates, birth certificates and ration cards.

Even earlier, the police had picked up Abdul Latif, an ISI agent. The hijackers passed on a message, via a Pakistani contact, to Latif in Mumbai on 29 December 1999, asking him to tip off a TV correspondent in London that the hijackers would blow up the plane if their demands were not met. Two Pakistanis, Mohammed Rehan of Karachi and Mohammed Iqbal of Multan, and a Nepalese citizen, Yusuf Nepali, were arrested.

In a lengthy statement on the Pakistani connection, shortly afterwards the investigations began, L.K. Advani pointed out, 'The hijack was an ISI operation, executed with the assistance of the Harkat ul-Ansar. All five hijackers were Pakistanis.' He said the preparations for the hijack began two months ago. Latif, recruited when he was in the Gulf and trained in Pakistan and Afghanistan, visited Kathmandu several times. On 1 November, he and Chief flew to Calcutta, took a train to New Jalpaiguri and then a bus to Kathmandu. Latif returned after dropping Chief off. On 1 December, Latif again went to Kathmandu with Shankar and returned to New Delhi on 17 December, after which he proceeded back to Mumbai.

Despite denials by Pakistan, the evidence is too overwhelming. The US apparently reprimanded General Pervez Musharraf, the

Pakistani dictator. The *New York Times* reported in early January 2000, 'The general was told that the United States believed that the Harkat was responsible for the hijacking and the United States believed the group operated openly and clandestinely with the support of the military and intelligence services in Pakistan.'

After the hijacking, many people have come to me and asked, 'Don't you wish you weren't a pilot?' I have to say they are right, or almost right. Of course, I love flying. There's a sense of pleasure involved. It's very beautiful flying through the clouds, feeling the surge of the engine. I don't think I'll ever tire of flying, though I have to say, one hijacking was quite enough.

Then they ask me how I had the stamina to fly to Kathmandu and then to Amritsar, Lahore, Dubai and Kandahar all in a day and a bit. I laugh and tell them that my stamina comes from driving tractors in between my flying lessons during my college days!

We must learn positive things from all experiences we undergo, and I think even the hijacking has helped me to become a better person. I think I am more confident now. Certainly, about my flying. If you've flown to Kandahar with a gun to your head, you can fly anywhere. Also, I have greater confidence in my ability to handle fear. I was tested by fire and not found wanting.

One of the other positive things that has come out of this experience is the respect I have earned. I have always been a private person. But now everyone comes to the cockpit to meet me when I am flying. I flew the Indian cricket team back from Calcutta recently. On the flight, they asked the air hostesses, 'Devi Sharan? The Devi Sharan of IC 814?'

I have also received a lot of fan mail and letters of appreciation from colleagues, which makes me feel both proud and humble. 'You have shown courage and bravery that's very rarely seen. You have done your duty under terrible mental stress, looking after your passengers despite your great physical distress... So here is what the Indian Airlines family want to do—stand up and salute you,' wrote V.S. Shirali, a colleague at Mumbai airport. Some other colleagues wrote, 'We were proud to have a commander of your caliber in our airlines. You were the unfortunate chosen one for the impossible mission but have successfully managed to come unscathed along with our crew.' Some of the passengers wrote to me too. One said, 'I was impressed by your coolness, your leadership, sense of humor and "ever-ready service culture" during those difficult days. It is impossible to imagine the kind of pressure on you at that time, but you kept us going until the last minute.' Such letters will always remain among my greatest treasures.

But I have been criticized too, and I feel somewhat unfairly. Shortly after the hijacking, Vishwa Hindu Parishad leader Ashok Singhal called me a coward. The Union Government wasn't short of courage, he told reporters, Captain Sharan was. 'The government does not have to demonstrate courage. If the pilot had the courage, he could have just refused to fly,' he said. 'We would not like a Hindu to be a coward. Nor would we want him to be a bully. We want to inculcate in him courage to protect the self-respect of the Hindus.'

This was an unexpected rebuke. I felt it was unjustified coming from someone who does not have any knowledge of aviation. Moreover, does he not know the value of human life? Even in the Mahabharata, Lord Krishna tried his best to avoid bloodshed. There is one question I would like to ask this gentleman. Did he meet the families of the passengers or crew during the crisis?

What touched me deeply was how the people who had been there reacted to these charges. Many passengers were quick to react. 'We would request Mr Singhal not to make statements which are insulting to courteous people like Captain Sharan...

had it not been for him, we would not have come back alive,' said Virendra Singh, Atul Gupta, and Gopal and Anita Agarwal.

Sanjeev Sharma, Romesh Grover and S. Kar were even more critical. 'Captain Sharan handled the hijackers very courageously. When the negotiations broke down, and the hijackers wanted the plane blown up in the air, he personally instructed many of us about how to open the plane's doors. He told us he would not take off but crash against a wall at the end of the runway to allow us a chance to open the doors and escape. He would have been killed in the process but didn't seem to care.'

I hope that the lessons from the hijacking will not be lost. It brought to light many of the problems and loopholes which exist in our security procedures. There are ways we can improve matters. I think there should be a final check when passengers climb on to the aircraft. Also, especially in India, too much cabin luggage is allowed. It would improve matters too if there was a new cadre of security staff for airports who are specially trained for the job, rather than having members of the police force who are not specialized in this. Also, there should be an airline policy on hijackings. Now, there is no set policy or training for cabin and cockpit crew for handling hijackers. So, everything we did was by instinct, but we would have felt so much more confident had we thought about such situations before.

What would I expect if another hijacking happens? Quicker reactions by the authorities, a responsible media, a trained crew able to recognize weapons and security men to act, if possible. I wonder if this is asking for too much. I know that lightning can strike the same place twice. My plane could again be hijacked someday...

Still, the IC 814 affair is over. Or is it? On 5 January, I was flying to Goa when the air hostess opened the cockpit door and entered. For a second, I was back on IC 814, flying over Uttar Pradesh and five hijackers in the plane.

I think for me, the decisive end to the affair came on 16 June 2000. I was going to fly to Kathmandu. Call it coincidence, call it whatever, but I found that I would be flying the same plane, the familiar weather-beaten EDW with chipped paint in the cabin and the blue-and-green sunshades. One of the air hostesses was also from the 24 December flight: Tara Debnath.

'Don't worry. Everything will be all right,' I told her though I needed reassurance myself.

I was nervous and sweaty. 'It is my work. It is my duty,' I kept repeating to myself. I had trouble walking to the aircraft.

The security men at New Delhi recognized me. 'This is the same pilot. He's going to Kathmandu,' one of them told the others. They were looking at me.

At Kathmandu, I noticed the new security arrangements. They were excellent. And then I was on the flight back to New Delhi: IC 814. On the way back, I didn't even notice when we passed the point we had been hijacked as I was too busy dealing with the difficult weather conditions. I remembered only after we passed Lucknow. In New Delhi, as we were getting off the plane, a passenger came up to me. 'You've brought the plane back to New Delhi today,' he said.

'Did you want to go to Kandahar?' I asked. As he turned pale, I laughed and walked off.

I don't know where Chief is. Or where the others are.

But I'll always remember those days and nights of terror.

WHERE THEY ARE TODAY

Captain Devi Sharan, continues to fly for Indian Airlines which is merged with Air India now. He was awarded the 1999 Conway Safe Skies Award, at Atlanta, Georgia, in recognition of his extraordinary efforts to protect international air travel from acts of terrorism. He lives in New Delhi with his wife and both daughters are senior pilots, married and settled in their family life.

Captain Rajinder Kumar is still with Indian Airlines which is merged with Air India now. He lives in Hyderabad. Mr Anil Jaggia retired from Indian Airlines on 29 February 2000. He wrote a book about the hijacking and passed away in November 2015.

Rajni Chandrashekhar, one of the bravest people on the plane, continues to be an air hostess. She is Hyderabad-based.

Rachna Katyal joined Indian Airlines as an assistant in the personnel department in New Delhi.

Ashok Kathuria, one of the passengers, continues to run his business in New Delhi. He has been to Kathmandu several times since the hijacking.

Maulana Masood Azhar, whose release was the main goal of the hijacking, now lives in Pakistan and continues his work as a leader of the Jaish-e-Mohammed, responsible for regularly pushing terrorists into Jammu and Kashmir. The Jaish were responsible for deadly attacks on the Pathankot airbase, in 2016, and in Pulwama, in 2019, when a suicide bomber killed over 40 Indian para-military personnel.

The hijackers drove down from Kandahar to Pakistan. Two unidentified gunmen killed Mistry Zahoor Ibrahim, one of the hijackers, in Karachi, in early 2022. Indian intelligence agencies said the others are living in Pakistan.